Love, Sex, and Lasting Relationships

Love, Sex, and Lasting Relationships

Chip Ingram

BakerBooks

A Division of Baker Book House Co
Grand Rapids, Michigan 49516

© 2003 by Chip Ingram

Published by Baker Books
a division of Baker Book House Company
P.O. Box 6287, Grand Rapids, MI 49516-6287
www.bakerbooks.com

Published in association with Yates & Yates, LLP, Literary Agents, Orange, California

Produced with the assistance of the Livingstone Corporation

Printed in the United States of America

ISBN 0-8010-1254-6

ISBN 0-8010-6475-9 (intl. pbk.)

Library of Congress Cataloging-in-Publication Data is on file at the Library of Congress, Washington, D.C.

I dedicate this book to Dave and Polly Marshall, who taught me by their lives and words how to do relationships God's way. Thank you, Dave, for modeling personal purity and integrity. Thank you for letting me watch you date your wife, even after you had four children. And thank you for listening to my struggles and even sharing a few of your own. My marriage and family are a part of your spiritual legacy for the glory of God.

Contents

Acknowledgments

Written during a traumatic time in our lives, I am deeply grateful for Neil Wilson's flexibility in helping me write and edit the project, Annette Kypreos's organizational skill and encouragement, Vicki Crumpton's patience and understanding, my wife's inspiration and modeling of these truths, and my children's feedback and endurance in hearing and critiquing me on multiple occasions. Finally, a special word of appreciation goes to the people of Baker Book House who have demonstrated a commitment to excellence and a commitment to get this message to all corners of our culture.

Introduction

Few subjects in life ignite as much passion and longing within us as our desire for love, our interest in sex, and our hope for enduring relationships. Regardless of our backgrounds, race, values, intelligence, or experience, we all long to be loved. Every human being on this planet craves to be that "cherished person" to someone else. In like manner, the mystery and the power of human sexuality draw us like an invisible magnet into the world of relationships.

Put simply, we humans are relational beings. We were made by God to love and be loved. We crave the intimacy, acceptance, security, and significance that flow when we bond in mind, heart, and body with a member of the opposite sex.

If you think I'm overstating the case, stop and think about your first reaction to the title of this book. What caught your attention? Why were you drawn to the picture of the couple on the cover, rubbing noses on a windswept beach? Did you read romance in their gaze? Did you catch the sense of intimacy and shared richness of their awesome relationship? Did you want to change places with one of them?

If so, I'll tell you why. That picture represents our longing. You want what that couple has, and so do I. It doesn't matter if you're seventeen or seventy-seven, the words *love, sex,* and *lasting relationships* evoke immediate and powerful responses within each of us. Pictures that capture that hope also capture our attention.

Let's face it. After taking care of the necessities of life like food, clothing, and shelter, most of us spend the bulk of our waking hours pondering, pursuing, or solving problems related to this area of life. I mean, stop for a moment and consider the songs that we listen to every day, songs like:

- "Can't Live without Your Love, Babe"
- "Ain't Got No Lovin'"
- "If Loving You Is Wrong, I Don't Want to Be Right"
- "I Wanna Hold Your Hand"
- "What's Love Got to Do with It?"

Add to these almost any other song on the current Top Forty list.

Day after day, people all over the globe, representing every nationality and language, sing about their desires for or their disappointment with love.

Walk through your local bookstore, if you're not standing in one right now, and check out the romance novels, the self-help section, or the relational resources rack. Notice how many volumes focus in one way or another on sex, romantic love, or how to have a great relationship. Or the next time you go grocery shopping, examine the glossy and glamorous magazines in the racks by the checkouts. Has *Cosmo* ever had a cover without the word "sex" on it? Who's on the front of *People, Globe, The Inquirer,* and *Star*? Aren't those publications filled with photos of who's together this week, who's rumored to have cheated on his or her mate, or what couples have joined the split list? Why

> Like it or not, we live in a world where *love, sex,* and *relationships* get top billing in the hearts and minds of nearly all of us.

do these magazines sell? Like it or not, we live in a world where *love, sex,* and *relationships* get top billing in the hearts and minds of nearly all of us.

Advertisers figured out long ago that our preoccupation with emotional connectedness and sex provides a great way to sell merchandise. Whether it's using sex to sell beer and cars during the timeouts of televised games or showing scenes from loving relationships while they are trying to convince us to change long-distance carriers, the underlying message remains constant—the key to happiness and fulfillment in life is all about *love, sex,* and *lasting relationships.*

Unfortunately, despite all the hype in magazines, movies, seminars, and books, for the most part people aren't doing very well when it comes to this area of their lives. The words divorce, breakup, wounds, baggage, ex-mate, and abuse are all too common in our relational vocabulary. Even in surviving marriages, the atmosphere often reeks of unhappiness and disappointment. We long to love and we long to be loved, but we just don't seem to know how to do it very well. And for all the talk and openness there is about sex today, sexuality still ranks as one of the persistent points of conflict in most relationships. It appears as if the greater the hunger for enduring love and lasting relationships, the shorter their lifespan. To paraphrase a song, love seems to end before it has begun.

So what's wrong here? Are we all destined to be frustrated and become the products and perpetrators of dysfunctional relationships? Or is there a better way? Is there, in fact, a secret, a plan, or a different paradigm for genuine love, great sex, and an enduring relationship?

Well, as presumptuous as it may sound, this book promises to deliver exactly that, not because I'm particularly smart or have the market cornered on these issues but because the one who created you to be loved and the one who made sex for your enjoyment has an understandable game plan for how relationships can and do work. The one who designed you to love and be loved has also provided specific wisdom and instructions to make that possible in your daily life. This book is about that wisdom—how it can and will work for you.

You might be thinking, *But why read this book? I'm single.* Or, *I'm divorced.* Or even, *I'm widowed. I'm not in a relationship right now. How in the world could these chapters be helpful for me?* Actually, this book is very much for singles, divorcees, and those who are widowed, as well as for those who are married. Regardless of your current relational status, if you don't understand romantic relationships from God's perspective, you are destined to a life of severe disappointment and significant frustration.

If you are in a significant relationship but not yet married, this book will help you assess your relationship's health, strength, and areas of need. You will learn how to build qualities into your relationship that will make it not only exciting but also able to last for the long haul. Wouldn't you like to arrive at the moment when you say, "I take you . . . until we are parted by death," and actually have a plan for how you will pull that off?

If you're single and not currently in a significant relationship, this book will save you boatloads of future heartache—and put some past hurts into perspective. It will help you avoid problems and habits that frequently sink relationships as well as show you how to construct and navigate your future relationship to sail with confidence and purpose. You'll learn to do relationships the way God intended.

In fact, this book's greatest value may be for people who are not yet in relationships. During a recent conference in the Midwest I taught the material in this book to several hundred college-age students. One student summed up what I heard from many: "Most of the time when people speak on relationships, you feel kind of 'out of it' if you're not dating someone. But this series was different. I'm not in a relationship right now, but these principles have been tremendously helpful for me as a single person who is considering what kind of relationship I want and how I want to go about it."

If you're married, this book will provide a reality check on your expectations. It will help direct your energy and focus toward the aspects of your relationship that will build increased joy and deeper intimacy. It will also help you address attitudes and practices in your marriage that may be putting relational road-blocks between you and your mate. As one couple shared with me privately, "It's amazing how much our culture talks about sex but how little my wife and I have ever really discussed its impact on our relationship." They were surprised when they compared their culture-based expectations about sex with God's perspective and prescription for enhancing sexual intimacy. The differences were remarkable!

If you are divorced, you'll find hope in these pages. This book will help you discover what may have gone wrong in your mar-riage and how to prepare yourself now to build healthy, positive relationships in the future. Unfortunately, people desperate for relationships tend to keep doing the very things that destroy those relationships. They've never heard that there really is a

> This book fits you, whoever and wherever you are.

better way. One man from Australia who had been divorced mul-tiple times heard the material in this book over the Internet and wrote me a grateful E-mail in which he said, "Chip, I finally get it. Hearing you speak on love, sex, and lasting relationships opened my eyes and gave me new hope. I identified with the people in your stories. Now I see how I set up my previous relationships for absolute failure. Thank you for putting me straight. I was about to make the same mistakes again!"

Getting letters, calls, and E-mails from people in each category I just described convinced me I needed to explore every way pos-sible to get these time-tested truths into people's lives. The book you're holding is part of that effort. It goes out with my prayer that a transformation and revolution will occur in your thinking about relationships as you read these chapters. I'm asking God to grant you insight and discernment to approach relationships as never before so that you can experience the awesome mystery of the lasting relationship that you deeply desire.

By the way, if you're already in a great marriage, congratu-lations! Read this book as a personal investment in your most important human relationship. Why? Three reasons. First, great marriages stay great with attention in the right places. Second, great marriages can get even better (that's one of the things that makes them great). Third, great marriages deserve to be copied. After you read this book, the next time someone asks you, "What's your secret? How do have such a great relationship?" you will have something to give them to read.

So this book fits you, whoever and wherever you are. Thousands of people have heard what you are about to read, and those who have applied these timeless truths have discovered that they work. The testimonies in scores of E-mails, letters, and faxes from our radio audience confirm that there really is hope for relationships! People are hungry for an alternative. If the way that most people are building their marriages is failing, doesn't it make sense to consider another way? Frankly, I'd rather not read or hear any more about the wreckage of marriages and relationships. I'd much rather be a part of making things better. I've seen enough pain in people's lives to last me for a long time. I've cried with too many broken people. So much of it could be avoided. There is hope! There is a better way to find love, stay in love, and grow in intimacy for a lifetime.

I share the material in these chapters with confidence. As you will notice, I'm certainly working on applying these truths in my own marriage. My wife and I know how *not* to do relationships, and by God's grace we've learned how a relationship can be transformed from unhappy drifting to intimate joy. I promise that if you will trust and implement this way of thinking about and doing relationships, yours can be deeply satisfying and lasting. These principles work not because they come from me but because they come from the One who designed you. Love, sex, and lasting relationships were all God's idea. He made you for relationship. He created that longing for connection with others that is such a part of your life. And because you are the object of his love and affection, he wants to fulfill these longings in ways beyond your wildest dreams.

I

Hollywood's Formula for Lasting, Loving Relationships

f you failed to read the Introduction, stop. Do not pass go.
Don't even think about collecting two hundred dollars.
Please turn back and read it now. The introduction of this
book sets the tone and focus for all that we are going to
talk about. This chapter will not help you in the way it's
intended to unless you quickly read the introduction to
grasp where we're headed and why.

We've made the point that love, sex, and lasting relationships
are among the most passionate desires of people's hearts. We've
also noted that most people are simply not experiencing love and
sexual intimacy to the degree or to the extent that they desire.
Despite all the songs about love, people don't seem to be getting
much of it. Despite all the movies that glorify sex, it remains one
of the most common points of frustration and the spark that sets
off arguments and fights in relationships. The vivid and passionate scenes on the screen or in romance novels rarely resemble the
actual relationships people experience. But we've said that there

is hope. God has provided specific instructions about how to nurture your love life, find the right mate, and develop a mutually satisfying and powerfully bonding sexual relationship. God knows the longings of your heart and wants to teach you how to build a relationship that actually gets better and better, and deeper and deeper, as the decades go by.

How's Your Love Life?

Let me ask you some questions.

- How's your love life?
- Where are you frustrated?
- What are you looking for but can't find?
- What's going well and what has you desperately confused?

Take a moment and think about these questions. Let down those defenses that you've used to block the pain of your past or the frustrations of your present. Conduct a brief inventory of your relational world. The purpose for pausing now, before you continue to read, has nothing to do with morbid introspection. I simply want you to stop and ponder your relationships. Take this opportunity to see, as clearly as possible, the present condition of your love life. I know I'm asking you to do something that isn't easy. Sometimes our most difficult struggle in a sensitive area like this comes when we try to really understand where we are in relation to others. Perhaps I can offer you some help in your personal reflection.

If I passed you on the street, what look would I see on your face and in your eyes? Would I see someone who is fearful, frantic, angry, or even disappointed? If I observed you for a few hours, would I note a remarkable lack of joy, contentment, or peace in your life? Would I sense that you feel like you're moving along through life but don't seem to be getting where you want to go? Would your daily routine, private conversations, and journal entries offer abundant clues that you are longing for love but you haven't found it yet?

Are you one of those young (or not-so-young) people who have been wounded deeply? Do you find yourself limping through life from the pain in your past? If so, please don't feel ashamed; you're not alone. In fact, as a result of counseling hundreds of people over the years, I'm no longer surprised when a majority of them sadly admit that their quest for love has left them wounded and scarred. Are you one of them? Unfortunately, most of us have grown up in families where love was poorly modeled and rarely discussed. Well over half of us have grown up in homes where we watched our parents seethe, fight, separate, and divorce, leaving us as emotional orphans. Now, as badly as we yearn for love, we are deeply afraid that it will simply bring more pain. Many admit to me privately that they are torn between their longing for love and their fear of the pain and rejection that it might bring. If we talked quietly over a cup of coffee, would you share these same fears and hurts?

> Now, as badly as we yearn for love, we are deeply afraid that it will simply bring more pain.

For others, it's not a matter of finding someone to love; it's more a matter of severe disappointment in the quality of the present relationship. Perhaps you find yourself in one of those marriages—traveling down the road of life together but rarely holding hands or talking to each other. Maybe you are a wife who looks with aggravation at your husband while he seems to stare at every woman on the road except you. Maybe you've spent years expecting your husband to become someone else. Perhaps you're a husband who secretly has been looking for something newer, better, and more exciting in your relationship. In this kind of relational pattern, both partners report dissatisfaction with each other. Neither seems to live up to the other's expectations. Does this sound all too familiar to you? Does this describe your relationship right now? You can be honest. My desire is in no way to open a wound or to drag you down but simply to help you clearly understand your starting point so that we can make real progress together in the pages ahead.

Or maybe what I've described so far doesn't fit you at all. Perhaps you are reasonably satisfied with the relationship that you are in and all seems to be going well, at least on the surface. People often assume that you're married, but when they press the issue, you report, "No, we're deeply in love but simply living together." And though the relationship seems to be going well right now, a closer look would reveal some secret fears that you have shared with almost no one. You live with a deep sense of uncertainty. It's expressed in those cautious glances at one another that calculate how much time you still have on the clock before the good feelings run out. It's the constant question that runs through the back of your mind: "If he really loves me, why would he avoid a long-term, exclusive commitment?" It's living with the reality that any day, at any moment, the other person can walk out because neither of you has made a permanent commitment to the other. The missing sense of security and permanence creates a void beneath your feet. Much of your energy goes into pleasing and appeasing your partner because of deep-seated fears that he or she will one day find someone else or grow tired of you. Those fears continually plague your emotional psyche. There are certain things you simply can't share. Certain protective inner walls always remain in place because, despite some very positive aspects to your relationship, you both know in your heart of hearts that this can end at any time. In most cases, such a relationship will run its course, and the couple will either choose to marry or they will drift apart. Does this describe you? Do you have nagging fears about where the relationship is going and where it will land? Is it possible that this "easy living arrangement" may feel good for the short term but fail to offer fertile soil for the enduring relationship you secretly desire?

Some of you reading this book have no need for a relational inventory. Your emotional and relational world is a raw, gaping wound. In fact, you still bear the tan line on your ring finger that shows you were married but now you walk alone. You've entered a new world—the world of "single again." It's strange, different, and uncomfortable. You look at other people, afraid they will notice the mixture of desperation and disappointment on your face. You try hard to find out what others are really like while carefully protecting and hiding your own real identity. You don't want to reveal too much too soon. You are still wounded by your broken relationship, yet you are driven by your need for love to find a special person whom you can cherish and who will cherish you.

Whichever of these people you identify with the most, you probably noticed that they share one characteristic. They're all looking for love in a particular way. Although we rarely think about it in this way, almost all of us follow a certain set of unwritten rules and make certain assumptions about relationships. But most of us have never really questioned where these rules or assumptions came from or why they are worth following. We move from relationship to relationship and often heartache to heartache with certain widely shared presuppositions about what love is, how to find it, and what to do when we don't have it. Unfortunately, our ideas about love and our methods for finding the love of our lives have rarely been thoroughly examined or evaluated. The rules about relationships are such a part of our culture that we hardly ever ask ourselves these important questions:

- "Am I going about finding love in a way that works?"
- "Am I going about developing this relationship in a way that builds intimacy, depth, endurance, and joy?"

To the contrary, most of us simply follow the rules as we go through life looking, seeking, and experimenting in our attempts to find love, sex, and lasting relationships.

What I'm about to share in this next section may be the most important ideas that you read in this book. I'm going to propose that the paradigm (the set of unwritten rules) about love that we have accepted is dysfunctional. In fact, I'm going to suggest that we've been unconsciously brainwashed into believing a number of false premises about how love, sex, and

hips develop. I'm not suggesting there has been
empt to ruin our lives, but I am emphatically
hinking about relationships has developed in
when examined, turns out to be incapable of
producing the kind of relationships
we're seeking.

Isn't it time that we reevaluate our
view of love and how it grows? Doesn't
it seem logical with so much relational
fallout, chaos, and pain that we stop
and ask ourselves, "Where did we get
our ideas about how relationships work?
Could it be that we are trying to find
something that doesn't exist, or are
we simply looking for it in the wrong
places and in the wrong ways?"

Where do you get most of your ideas
about love? What are your sources of
information about love, sex, or lasting
relationships? Before we move forward, let's go back to the starting point and take a closer look at the unwritten rules we have
unconsciously accepted as true. Let's examine together where we
get our ideas about love.

> A way of thinking
> about relationships
> has developed in our
> culture that, when
> examined, turns out
> to be incapable of
> producing the kind
> of relationships
> we're seeking.

Where Do We Get Our Ideas about Love?

I can certainly imagine a world in which children grow up
surrounded by good examples of loving relationships. I can see
mothers and fathers openly sharing affection, keeping love alive,
and talking with their kids about every aspect of relationships. I
can picture father-son and mother-daughter moments when they
gradually share age-appropriate insights about love and sexuality.
But did anything like that ever happen to you? Did your mom or
dad ever sit down with you and say, "This is how to build a healthy
relationship with the opposite sex"? Did wise and trusted adults
ever tell you, "This is what sex is really all about" beyond the phys-

ical details you got in a ninth-grade health class? Were you ever in a warm, positive, family conversation in which you heard, "This is why and how sex can be beautiful, good, and wonderful, but be careful, because this is how sex can be distorted and destructive"? Did your parents ever have a discussion with you about how to build intimacy in a relationship through communication, commitment, and clear, shared goals?

The answer for most of us is no. No one ever gave us reliable guidelines for these personal areas of our lives. Most of us learned about love, sex, and relationships through our culture. Our teachers, sadly, have been older teens who themselves came from dysfunctional homes. If that isn't enough, the media have sold us a false bill of goods with regard to the entire notion of love, sex, and relationships. After listening to thousands of songs and getting a daily dose of television, movies, and romance novels, our hearts and minds have been filled with false ideas about what love, sex, and relationships are all about.

Taken together, all these songs, TV programs, movies, and books have instilled in us a definite prescription about how love, sex, and relationships are supposed to work. You and I have spent countless hours singing along with popular songs, following television programs, and anticipating the next sequel of our favorite movie hero. In the process we have become unconsciously convinced that if we follow a simple, four-step approach to relationships, it will work out for us just like it works in the movies or like it says in the song. Now don't get me wrong. I don't mean that all the writers of songs, movies, and books got together to come up with a specific four-step approach. But I do mean that if you analyze the songs, movies, and books that fill our lives, you will see emerging from them a clear-cut and consistent set of assumptions about relationships. Whether intended or not, Hollywood has a formula for love, sex, and lasting relationships. However, once we carefully examine this formula, we may decide it could be better described as "Hollywood's Formula for Sex, Love, and Losing Relationships." If you think I'm overstating the case, keep your own views of love and sex in mind as I give you an overview of Hollywood's formula. Ask yourself if this formula doesn't in fact promise that you can be deeply loved, have awesome sex, and walk into the sunset with another person for life if you simply do what happens in the movies.

The Hollywood Formula

Let's look at what Hollywood says makes a successful relationship. I've eliminated the lighting, the warm scenes, walking on the beach hand in hand, the slow-motion moments, and the rising and falling of background music. I've just cut to the chase.

There are basically four steps, according to Hollywood, that lead to deep, intimate, sizzling relationships that will last forever.

Step 1: Find the Right Person

That's right. The key to love is finding that one special person who was made just for you. She's out there; you just have to find her. Drive around. Hang out. Be on the lookout. The moment will come. Do you remember the scene from the movie *While You Were Sleeping* when Sandra Bullock finds her "right one" when he steps up to her subway counter and asks for a ticket to Connecticut? Then he gets knocked senseless, and while she's visiting him in the hospital she just happens to meet his brother who turns out to be her real "right one." In *Sweet November* Keanu Reeves tries to cheat on his driver's exam, gets Charlize Theron in trouble, and meets the love of his life instead. James Bond usually meets his "right ones" when they are trying to kill him. Jennifer Lopez meets one Mr. Right when he saves her from being run over by a dumpster in one movie, then finds the love of her life when she's the maid cleaning up his hotel room in her next film.

Do you get the picture? Whether it's the movies and stars of today or the Clark Gables, Cary Grants, Marilyn Monroes, or Raquel Welches of the past, the message is always the same. Finding the right person just happens! It's wild, accidental, and you're helpless in the process. Eventually you're going to meet the "right one." When you least expect it, expect it. Right around the next corner you will find someone much better than anyone you have ever known. True love is mystical and magical. It's all about finding the right person. If it can happen to J. Lo, it can happen to you. Just keep looking.

Step 2: Fall in Love

When you find that person, something will snap and you'll just know. No one knows how, but you'll just know. Something about the way she walks or talks. A brief look or gesture may be enough. You may not know her name or much about her, but you will know that you have fallen in love. In *Sleepless in Seattle* Tom Hanks just needs his little boy to get on the radio and tell the nation the sad story of his father's life, and Meg Ryan soon knows she loves this man. When they finally meet against all odds at the top of the Empire State Building, all it takes is one look and two strangers instantly fall in love. Is it the music? The altitude? Or just the script? Or, as they say, is it just that old magic called love?

In the movies you can fall in love with strangers and it's the real thing. In the Hollywood formula, love is based on chemistry, not knowledge or character. According to our pop culture's concept of love, you can sing, "Hello, I love you, won't you tell me your name?" with a straight face. You'll be sure you're in love because you'll have "ooey gooey" feelings and electrical pulses will surge all over your body. Unfortunately, your IQ will drop about thirty points immediately. You'll spend money you don't have. You'll spend time doing things that are ridiculous. This amazing, much-sought-after experience of "falling in love" is equated with overwhelming feelings that discount reason, background, shared interests, or compatibility. Love, says Hollywood, "makes you crazy." You'll make decisions about which everyone who knows you would say, "That's the dumbest thing you've ever done." But you're in love. And love is all that matters. And you know it because emotions this strong, this sudden, and this overwhelming must be the real thing. The only choice seems to be to take the next step.

Step 3: Fix Your Hopes and Dreams on This Person for Your Future Fulfillment

In the movies love vetoes every other decision. Brides and grooms are regularly left at the altar because their future mates have decided to run off with someone else with whom they are "really in love." Once you fall in love, in the Hollywood version, every other promise you have made is null and void. You can't be held to any previous commitment. The person with whom you "fall in love" will become the object of your life, your future, your dreams, and your satisfaction. You have suddenly realized that he and he alone will make you complete. He will make you whole. Life will have meaning like it never has before (except for all the other times you've been in love). In fact, you will find yourself living and thinking the lines from your favorite songs: "I don't know what I'd do without you" and "I can't go on without you, baby." You begin to believe you can't make it without him or her. You constantly daydream about this person, writing perfect, romantic scripts about your future life together. You fully expect that this person will be able to meet your deepest longings and needs and come through for you 100 percent of the time. Though we all intellectually know it is impossible, we have been subtly taught to base our future happiness on the unconscious expectation that finding the right person will solve all our problems.

> Hollywood equates infatuation with love.

Hollywood equates infatuation with love. This period of intense infatuation and supercharged emotions can last anywhere from six weeks to eighteen months. And when the feelings start to subside (as they always do), we've been brainwashed to conclude that our love is dying. The perfect partner turns out to have a flaw or two. She can't quite live up to our imagination. Relational conflict begins to raise its ugly head. Dissatisfaction gradually erodes those once euphoric feelings. Disillusioned and discouraged, we begin to change our focus. As emotions wane and irritations arise, we start to blame our problems on the other person's inability to measure up.

Hollywood provides a convenient "Plan B" when "true love" falters. Clichés abound to describe how we've "drifted apart" or are "falling out of love" or how good it once was, but it's "just not the same anymore." We're led to believe that "falling out of love" is an expected and natural risk in relationships. We either chose the wrong person or we were right for each other for a season but that season has now passed. Our lack of love has nothing to do with us; it is simply the result of discovering that we no longer have the right person in our life. And, since this happens all too often, the Hollywood formula has a fourth step that has become the norm in American life.

Step 4: If Failure Occurs, Repeat Steps 1, 2, and 3

Step 3 usually leads to failure, eventually. When relational breakdown occurs, the Hollywood formula offers a quick and supposedly painless solution: Take step 4; go back to the beginning. Repeat steps 1, 2, and 3. It's time once again to (1) **find the right person,** (2) **fall in love,** and (3) **fix your hopes and dreams on this new, improved person you have found.** This time maybe it will work. Just go on to the next partner, repeating steps 1–3.

You see, here is the premise behind the Hollywood formula: **The key to love is finding the right person.** If your current relationship isn't working, if for some reason this person doesn't fulfill all your dreams and desires, if you're not exhilarated, then you must have the wrong person. He may have seemed to be the right one at the start, but the fact that the feelings have faded means that he wasn't actually the right person for you. Throw that one away and find a new one. When you do, repeat the same formula until you get it right.

I know what I've shared sounds blunt and includes more than a little satire. But the fact remains: The books, movies, songs, and television programs that have become a common part of our thinking and vocabulary are consistently telling you and me that the way to love, sex, and lasting relationships is found through the four steps that I've outlined. It may sound harsh and burst a few romantic bubbles, but this Hollywood four-step formula is what most of us now unconsciously believe about how relationships work. It's the basis on which we approach our sexuality. It's how we evaluate whether our relationship is working or not. And if this formula is flawed and dysfunctional, as I will suggest, our basic thinking about relationships must change if we are ever to discover and enjoy the kind of love, sex, and lasting relationships that God has in mind for us.

Before you conclude that I've been a bit too harsh with Hollywood's formula, let's do a quick review of how the Hollywood formula is working in America today.

Report Card on the Hollywood Formula

I know it may threaten some of our most cherished assumptions about love, but let's take a candid look at the success rate of the Hollywood formula. How is it playing out in the lives of those who are putting it to the test?

> Sadly, we not only deny the rampant presence of divorce in our society, we also work hard to cover up the devastating effects.

The divorced population is the fastest growing marital category in the United States. In 1970 the total number of divorced people was 4.3 million. By 1996 (twenty-six years later) it was 18.3 million.[1] If we were talking about a virus or infection, the CDC (Centers for Disease Control) would be calling this a catastrophic epidemic. But this is far more serious than simply the miserable failures of "consenting adults." Not only is the Hollywood formula spectacularly unsuccessful, it also causes almost immeasurable pain, fallout, and damage.

Sadly, we not only deny the rampant presence of divorce in our society, we also work hard to cover up the devastating effects. What we hear, despite all the violence, anger, and bitter talk that echoes from divorce court, is, "We're still friends; it was just a mistake" or "Our kids know that we love them and still care for each other (even though we can't stand to live together anymore)." That's how divorce is treated in public. Unfortunately, the louder we shout "no-fault" or "friendly" divorce, the longer we cover up the damages. Research in the United States indicates that the pain, fallout, and damage go beyond the children. After a divorce, one-third of all women find themselves living at or below the poverty level at some time in their lives. Fractured relationships between in-laws and friends affect ever-widening circles and continue throughout life.

Not long ago, Judith Wollerstein wrote an article in *USA Weekend* titled, "Children of Divorce, Twenty-Five Years Later."[2] In it she described a landmark new study that has tracked children of divorce for twenty-five years. The study has found that the negative impact of family breakup continues well into adulthood. One such grown child of divorce reported, "Part of me is always waiting for disaster to strike. I live in dread that some terrible loss will change my life." That is what divorce sounds like twenty-five years later among those it hits hardest.

The article goes on to quote Mavis Hetherington, a divorce researcher and now professor of marital psychology at the University of Virginia, "In the short term, divorce is always troublesome for children." She has videotaped and scrutinized the workings of fourteen hundred divorced families since the early 1970s. She pinpoints a crisis period of about two years in the immediate aftermath of separation when adults, preoccupied with their own lives, typically take their eyes off their parenting duties at the very time when their children are reeling from their loss. Is it surprising that people are not emotionally attached in our day? Could this be the reason that in the last ten years instead of men marrying about age 23 and women about age 20, men are now marrying about age 27 to 28 and women about age 23? Does it surprise us that cohabitation has quadrupled? Do you hear what this generation is saying by their actions and sometimes admitting by their words?

- "I don't know if I believe in marriage."
- "I get close to someone, then the same thing always happens. I'm scared to death to make a commitment."

- "I don't know how marriage is supposed to work, but I know I grew up in a family where it didn't."
- "I've got unresolved issues and unresolved pain and a lot of fear about relationships."
- "I want intimacy and I long to be connected with someone else, but my heart got ripped out and no one helped me cope with the pain. They said I'd get over it. Well, I'm not over it. I'm afraid to go into new relationships."
- "The models that I had didn't work, and I've got mixed feelings about Mom and Dad. I was two days with one parent and two weeks with the other, summers in one house and school years in another. They kept asking me to choose who I wanted to stay with. Why couldn't they choose to stay together?"

And the pain goes on and on and on.

Yet Hollywood continues to promote its promise: Find the right person, fall in love, and put your hopes and dreams in him or her. If it doesn't work, it's not a big deal. Just find someone else. In fact, in some movies and songs, the message appeals directly to those already in relationships. If you find someone else and you're still married, you say, "If loving you is wrong, well, I don't want to be right." Yet hidden beneath the catchy words and tune you will discover a philosophy that promises new love but only delivers destruction. What starts out "feeling so right" ends up being so wrong.

> We keep doing the same thing in relationship after relationship, and it keeps producing the same tragic results.

Unless we consciously seek an alternative, we simply end up following the prevailing culture around us. That culture is saturated with Hollywood's formula. We sing along with the formula hits. We read about it; we watch it, and unconsciously almost all of us have bought into it to one degree or another. I find the Hollywood formula just as prevalent among Christians as among non-Christians. And the results are equally disastrous. We keep doing the same thing in relationship after relationship, and it keeps producing the same tragic results. We wouldn't accept the same results in other areas of life, so why do we accept them in this most important area of our lives? For example, if you place your thumb on a hard surface, grab a hammer, and hit your thumbnail firmly, it'll hurt badly. If you've never done that before, you may wonder if there is a correlation between the pain and the hammer hitting your thumb. So to verify your findings, you raise the hammer and smash your thumb again. That's probably more than enough to reach a lasting conclusion.

But when it comes to the Hollywood formula, we seem to refuse common sense. It's like taking a hammer and smashing relationships one after another and saying, "I guess I just had the wrong finger. Let's try another." Over and over we bring upon ourselves unbelievable pain. Do you know how God feels when a marriage disintegrates? Do you know how God feels as kids are torn apart when moms and dads split? Do you know how God feels when he sees the pain, rejection, and loneliness people experience following broken relationships? God weeps with compassion. But God doesn't simply stand idly by; he wants to help. He wants people to know that he has a better way and a better plan for them and their relationships. Far from the cookie-cutter formula of Hollywood that promises love and delivers pain, God has a prescription for love, sex, and lasting relationships. God created a plan especially designed for us to enjoy the highest and best with the opposite sex. Hollywood's formula is a poor Plan B. God has a Plan A that really works.

So where are you in your love life? How much of Hollywood's formula have you unconsciously bought into in your pursuit of love? Are you satisfied with the results of Hollywood's Plan B formula, or are you ready for Plan A?

Although we are not going to forget about Plan B throughout the rest of this book, our intention is to focus on Plan A. I believe with all my heart that if you understand God's original plan for relationships and have a clear idea of how that plan can work in your life, the superficial appeal of Hollywood's Plan B will evaporate. Hollywood's formula is broken! It does not deliver! It's time to stop, evaluate, and chart a new course toward meaningful love, intimate sex, and lasting relationships.

Personal Evaluation

Please take a moment, before you continue this book, to consider the following questions. They have been designed to allow you to personalize the truth we have been considering in this chapter.

1. How would you describe the effects of the Hollywood formula on your own life and relationships?

2. Which step of Hollywood's formula has produced the most significant area of hidden struggle in your life? Why? Following are the four steps with the effect that each is likely to produce:

1. *Find the right person.* You're always "on the lookout."
2. *Fall in love.* You find yourself strongly attracted to people who are practically strangers.
3. *Fix your hopes and dreams on that person.* You spend hours in fantasies, imagining a perfect life with someone you hardly know but are sure would be everything you need in a partner.
4. *Start over.* You can see a pattern of failed dreams or even failed relationships that indicates you have accepted the assumption that problems, struggles, and waning emotions mean you no longer have the right person in your life.

3. What in your relational life causes you the most concern or dissatisfaction? Explain. Following is a list of some potential areas of concern:

A. Lack of prospects—you want a deep loving relationship but don't seem to be meeting the kind of person who could fulfill that desire.
B. Lack of depth in communication—your current relationship is superficial, times of in-depth and honest sharing are infrequent or nonexistent.
C. Lack of passion—the sexual and affectionate aspects of your relationship seem stale, boring, infrequent, or nonexistent.
D. Lack of commitment—you do not hear, sense, or feel that your partner has made an irrevocable commitment to you and the relationship. Jealousy, fears, and insecurities frequently characterize your private thought life.

4. How would you describe your level of interest in finding an alternative to Hollywood's formula and getting specific, practical help with what you identified as your greatest concern in question 3?

2

Two Models
for Lasting Relationships

The room was packed and my palms were sweaty. Sitting before me were between eighty and a hundred people who recently had gone through the trauma of divorce. I didn't know most of them. They had come from all over the area and every conceivable background to an eight-week divorce recovery program that had gained a reputation as the place to get real help when one's relational world was shattered. Some came on the recommendation of friends. Others came under the somewhat stronger encouragement of a local judge who admonished those who passed through his divorce court to get help.

I was the senior pastor of the church in which they were meeting. My assignment had me speaking during the sixth weekly session. I glanced down at the title of my notes: "Growing through Divorce." The people looking at me had spent the last five weeks working through their feelings of pain, rejection, guilt, anger, and failure. They had begun to process what went wrong in their marriages and what part of the failure they needed to own. By this point, they were even wrestling with the issue of forgiveness—why it was such a difficult, but essential, first step in building a new life for themselves. They had listened to lectures, done homework, and shared their journey in small groups. Standing before them, I found it hard to read their faces. They had been told I would give them some very practical help. Looking into their eyes, I thought they did not look like they expected it.

I knew three facts about my audience. First, most of them were not Christians. Second, nearly all of them had completely bought into the Hollywood formula for love, sex, and lasting relationships. Many of them had worked through the formula more than one time. And third, the last thing they wanted to hear from this minister was judgmental preaching about their messed-up lives.

I began by explaining to them that I understood their pain and that I was there to help them, not preach at them. I made it clear that I believed only God had the real answers to their relational problems but tried to assure them that I would not be pushy or judgmental in my comments. During these introductory words I could see the discomfort in their shifting and challenging looks. Several deliberately crossed their arms in an unmistakable declaration that they didn't believe a word I said about "understanding their pain." Some even seemed to cringe in anticipation of the harsh and shaming message they were confident I would shell out.

I introduced my wife, Theresa, and we simply shared our story with the group. I described how both of us grew up in non-Christian homes. We had learned to do relationships like most people, absorbing the cultural clues and unwritten rules along the way. When we tried to live out of that relationship scheme, it didn't seem to work for either of us. I dated lots of girls throughout college and into my early twenties, always looking for "the right person." Instead, I managed to pile up a lot of emotional baggage and pain with each disappointing breakup. I know I also inflicted a lot of pain on others. I gained plenty of experience on how *not* to do relationships and little understanding of how to do them the right way.

At this point, Theresa began to recount her story. As soon as she began describing her first marriage, the crowd realized something was up. They sensed that we were not about to tell them a fairy tale. The tone in my wife's voice told them that she had already walked the path that was so familiar to them. Theresa told of the struggles of marrying right out of college, putting a husband through college, and the tentative relief and joy of a pregnancy with twins. Then she shared with them the shock, confusion, and pain of being suddenly abandoned by her husband for another woman shortly before the children were born. She recalled the added rejection and humiliation in the discovery that her mate had been unfaithful for well over a year. Her voice conveyed the repeated wounds caused by unsuccessful efforts at reconciliation. Her husband had left town with the other woman and moved to a different state. Her marriage was over—shattered into pieces that didn't make sense. What about the efforts to build and save the marriage? What about the love? What about the children? How could there be such deceit, such unawareness, such cold hardness against any gesture of peace or understanding?

> Heads nodded and tears flowed as Theresa openly shared the depth of her hurt and the extent of her loneliness and rejection.

The people seated before her didn't need any more details; they knew very well the place of despair that she had reached. She had staked her hopes, dreams, and future in another person who had proven completely unworthy of her trust. Heads nodded and tears flowed as Theresa openly shared the depth of her hurt and the extent of her loneliness and rejection. When she reached this point of her story, she paused for a few moments. From where I sat I could see the entire room. During her silence, the questions began to rise in the eyes of the audience: "So, then what happened?" "You're here now. How did that come to be?" "How did you get past what I don't believe I will ever get past?" "How did you survive?"

Without changing her tone Theresa picked up her account. Her despair led her to search for God. At first she simply found herself wondering if he even existed. She straightforwardly recounted the pain of her journey and how Christ had revealed himself to her in a tiny country church in West Virginia. She didn't report any instantaneous changes or quick fixes but a powerful peace and hope that gave her life a new direction. As she unfolded her experience, a spirit of hope seemed gradually to infiltrate the group. Even those who had been so obviously resistant earlier now hung on every word. She quietly described finding someone who would never leave her, who would never let her down, who would always love her, and who assured her of a wonderful plan for her future.

I guess she noticed a lot of people were glancing at me, so she added with a smile, "This was quite a while before I even met Chip." They chuckled. She continued, "At the lowest point in my life, when I had nothing to offer in return, Jesus walked into my world as my Savior and friend." She described the ways in which God became so personal and loving to her that he filled the void left by her husband and became a father to her children. Christ changed her view of herself and her view of the world. He altered the way she approached relationships. Then, again with a smile, she said, "And then four years later, he led Chip and me together."

As Theresa finished speaking and I prepared to step up to the podium, I could tell that the atmosphere in the room had changed dramatically. The listeners had gone from an unresponsive, suspicious group to one that hoped we were telling the truth. In the next few minutes, we shared a little about the more than twenty-five years that have passed since those events. We told them how those twin boys have grown up to be quality, godly young men. We described our own vibrant love and the deep relationship we gradually have developed despite all our past baggage. As we talked, another transformation came over the audience. They leaned toward us, expectantly. The quiet room became so intense I wasn't sure they were breathing. Their faces and body language seemed to cry out, "Tell me how. How can you come from such a shattered and dysfunctional past yet really find authentic love, intimate sex, and a lasting relationship?"

At that moment, I knew they were ready to hear about the radical differences between Hollywood's formula and God's prescription for love, sex, and lasting relationships. But, rather than embark on a lecture spelling out the four steps of the Hollywood formula, I asked them two simple, penetrating questions.

How do you go about finding real love?
Where did you learn your approach?

I wish I could have taken a picture of the blank looks on their faces. They didn't have a clue. By now, I've gotten used to seeing such looks every time I ask a group these questions. Perhaps you're wearing that same look at this moment.

It was obvious that they, like most of us, had never thought much about how they actually went about finding love. They certainly didn't know, offhand, where they'd learned it. Their bewilderment simply confirmed what we said about Hollywood's formula in the last chapter; it's a set of unwritten rules that has so permeated our culture and thinking that we don't even know where it came from.

I walked over to a white board and began drawing the diagram you will find below. The upside-down pyramid represents the starting point and the sequence of steps we take in seeking a love relationship with the opposite sex.

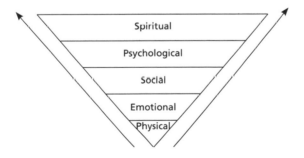

Without alluding to Hollywood's formula by name yet, I candidly described how most of us unconsciously learned to do relationships. I'm sure the group was a bit taken aback by my "just put it out there" openness, but why mince words when it's how we all learned to operate anyway?

The Physical Phase

When I finished drawing the diagram on the board, I put my finger on the point of the triangle and began to describe the process. "This is where we were taught to begin—with the physical." I wrote the word and explained, "We look for that babe or that hunk. It's all about chemistry and attraction. As men, we notice the tight sweater, the clingy skirt, and the glimpse of cleavage. The basis of our entire way of finding real love boils down to the physical." I sensed that the men were tracking with me 100 percent. Then I added, "And, though women were not quite as guilty of such a narrow perspective in the past, times have changed. The 'Hunk Factor' has moved beyond a strong chin, dreamy eyes, and a good build to the snug jeans and pleasing-posterior tests many women apply today." Several women's body language confirmed that they indeed were as interested in physical appearance as any man in the room.

> In our culture, physical appearance and sex appeal are paramount.

I continued, "If sparks fly, we move ahead. If not, we keep looking. In our culture, physical appearance and sex appeal are paramount. First encounters or dates often involve kissing and close physical contact, frequently leading to practical strangers sleeping together. If the experience is positive for both parties, the couple moves on to the next phase, building an emotional connection." So far, so good. I was describing a way of looking at life that they recognized as their own.

The Emotional Phase

After writing the word "emotional" on the board, I continued by explaining that the emotional phase marks the onset of euphoric feelings known as infatuation and often called "falling in love." Each person in the couple begins to see the other as the almost single focus of life. Emphasis in the relationship revolves around time together and physical expressions of love. Because of the intensity of positive feelings in this phase, the couple often avoids talking about the relationship itself. They are enjoying the emotions too much to talk about the relationship or where it is going. This phase, precariously balanced on a physical foundation, also tends to be filled with mood swings. Wild adoration can be followed almost instantaneously by insane jealousy. Because so little is actually known about the other person, statements he makes or actions she does are interpreted by the other person's own experiences and attitudes.

Here and there in the crowd I could see mental lights coming on. They had never reviewed their experiences with this perspective in mind. I continued, "Some couples quickly develop a breaking-up-and-making-up cycle in their relationship that creates special difficulties as the couple moves into the next expected phase of the formula—the social phase."

The Social Phase

I pointed to that section of the diagram and commented, "This next phase in building relationships according to our unwritten code involves the partners being drawn into one another's social circles. They meet each other's family and close friends."

Someone in the crowd inadvertently whispered, loud enough for everyone to hear, "Oh, yeah!" A ripple of chuckles instantly crossed the room. They remembered the danger signals.

When the laughter died down, I continued. "You're right. In this setting, the couple typically gets warm approval or dire warnings from the other people in their lives. Sometimes the warnings are heeded, but usually the couple simply moves forward no matter what kind of signals they get from others. After all, nothing can offer a more certain guide to the 'rightness' of their relationship than how they feel about each other." They were nodding in agreement.

The Psychological Phase

"But, about this time," I continued, "the couple also begins to enter a phase they can't really control but which affects the relationship—the psychological phase." I explained that in this phase, the stresses of life and the varied experiences created by the physical, emotional, and social aspects of the relationship create certain questions and needs in the relationship. It becomes time to talk about the future and explore in detail each other's personality and values. No matter how carefully they have guarded their character and personalities in the earlier phases of the relationship, time and closeness occasionally allow them to see the other as a "real" person. Flaws and potential problems begin to surface. The fragile nature of the relationship becomes clear. It doesn't take much for the relationship, balanced on such a small tip of physical attraction, to fall over and disintegrate. The possibility of disaster spurs the partners to consider alternatives.

> No matter how carefully they have guarded their character and personalities in the earlier phases of the relationship, time and closeness occasionally allow them to see the other as a "real" person.

If things continue along the normal pattern, one or both partners begin to long for a sense of permanence and exclusivity in the relationship. Moving in together as a vague trial period has become practically the norm today, but nothing replaces the desire to marry, which springs from that inner longing for the security of belonging together for life. I suspect that the popularity of elaborate, budget-busting, spare-no-expense weddings turns out to be one more attempt to create quickly and spectacularly what can only be truly accomplished with thoughtfulness and time. This desire to marry and mark the event with all the traditional trappings leads us to the final step in the relationship cycle—the spiritual phase.

As I walked to the board to write the title of that final step in the typical progression of relationship development, I sensed I had the group's undivided attention. Most of them were nodding in agreement as we moved from point to point. Many looked at each other in sudden realization that the room was filled with people who had something else besides divorce in common—most of them had taken the same steps to get there. This shared misery created a new sense of camaraderie. They began to laugh at some of the stories I told about my own life and the hindsight that shed so much light on the built-in pitfalls of the Hollywood formula. Some of them even mouthed their identification with some of the mistakes I talked about, "Yeah, been there—done that!"

The Spiritual Phase

I wrote the word "spiritual" in the top, widest section of the diagram. I said, "When a couple reaches the point where they yearn for the relationship to last, or they become sufficiently afraid it might end if they don't do something to give it long-term stability, they enter a phase we'll call 'spiritual.'" I pointed out that even those who have had little religious background and make no claim to follow Christ seem to know instinctively that they are about to participate in some kind of sacred moment. They want a pastor, priest, or rabbi to confirm their union and make it official. In a pinch, even a judge will do. A lovely church festooned with candles and flowers and a ceremony filled with solemn words spoken before friends and family create a religious veneer that is supposed to declare to the world that this relationship will last forever.

The audience members shook their heads thoughtfully. They knew differently. They understood that under all the extravagance of many weddings hides the sad truth that the couple at the altar is already in relational trouble. Many of them realized that their weddings had been unconscious, last-ditch efforts to save relationships that were already dying. They had been unable to handle all the complexity that was gradually crushing that initial carefree moment of "falling in love."

I knew that the next few minutes were crucial. "Let's face it," I said. "Most of us have attempted to find love, sex, and lasting relationships following the steps I just described. And many of us have discovered that the formula doesn't work. We've been almost convinced by repeated heartache and disappointment that this formula doesn't deliver what we want.

"Now, I realize that some of you have tried to break out of the system by avoiding it entirely. You want to withdraw from the world so you won't get hurt again. Your theme song is 'I'll Never Fall in Love Again' or 'Bye, Bye, Love.'" That got a few smiles and sheepish nods. "Many others have tried to keep the 'falling in love' part and eliminate everything else." I let that statement sink in for a moment and then asked, "Does that work?"

An instant chorus of whispered responses reached my ears. "No!"

I continued, "As I begin to explain the real alternative, please think about this: Maybe our problem isn't with the parts of the process we just described; maybe our problem lies in the fact that we have them completely out of order."

I walked over to a different white board and wrote at the top, "The Hollywood Formula." I turned and faced the crowd again and said, "I've entitled what I'm about to share 'The Hollywood Formula' because I believe that what we have come to believe about the ways in which we pursue love, sex, and lasting relationships has been largely shaped and encouraged by the media. I asked you earlier to tell me where you learned to do relationships the way you do them. Most of you honestly didn't know. I'm about to suggest a formula that I'm convinced will show you exactly where you learned about love."

I quickly outlined for them the same unwritten rules you read about in chapter 1. "This," I said, "is the formula we unquestioningly believe will lead us to love, sex, and lasting relationships, if we just apply it in our lives."

1. Find the right person.
2. Fall in love.
3. Fix all your hopes and dreams on that one person.
4. If failure occurs, repeat steps 1, 2, and 3.

I could tell they were with me. I also sensed their growing pain and desperation. Their faces were now easy to read. "Yes," their eyes and posture told me, "this is the way I've always done it, and I agree it doesn't work. But if there's a different way, a better way, tell me now because I don't think I can survive going through that cycle one more time!"

We now were simply a group of broken fellow travelers that had reached a common agreement. No more glitzy man-made formulas for love propagated by the silver screen. The audience members were ready to consider seriously a better way to do relationships. They were open to hear about a divine prescription that, if faithfully followed, would produce exactly the opposite results from what they had already experienced in their quest for love, sex, and lasting relationships.

God's Prescription for Lasting Relationships

I moved to the third white board and wrote at the top, "God's Prescription for Lasting Relationships." I turned and walked over to where Theresa was sitting at the end of the front row. Her earlier words of hope had struck a chord that the listeners still hoped would ring true for them.

Pointing to the third board as my other hand rested on Theresa's shoulder, I said, "What Theresa and I discovered, early in our relationship, is that God has actually given us a different order for these steps. The first way you can see this is by taking the triangular diagram you copied a few minutes ago and turning it upside down. Here's the lesson: God's prescription for relationships is the exact opposite of Hollywood's. It has a different starting place, it keeps a different focus, and it follows a different path. And, believe me, it achieves remarkably different results!"

Back at the third board, I sketched the triangle again, as you see it below:

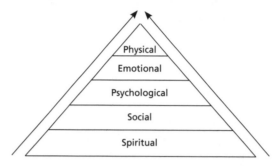

For the next thirty minutes I explained a revolutionary method for finding, developing, and sustaining a lasting relationship. I told the group how badly God wants this for each one of us and that cooperating with his design is the only true way to find what they had been looking for all their lives. I reminded them again that our problem isn't with the parts of the formula most of us follow in developing relationships; our problem really lies in the fact that we have them completely out of order.

The revolutionary method begins by establishing that a spiritual component is the only foundation broad and strong enough to sustain the rest of the relationship. This spiritual component includes a clear understanding of God's entire prescription for love, sex, and lasting relationships. I also reminded them several times (after the second or third, they began to laugh each time I mentioned it) that I had promised not to be "pushy" or "preachy" with them. The place we have to look when we want to understand what God says about anything is the Bible. "Would you allow me," I asked, "to simply give you a statement from the

> God's prescription for relationships is the exact opposite of Hollywood's.

Bible that will get us started in understanding God's prescription?" Enough of them immediately nodded, so I continued, "Ephesians 5:1–2 provides one of the clearest summaries of the revolutionary relational approach God wants us to take in loving others. In more ways than I can say in the time I have tonight, these words describe the prescription God applied to Theresa's life, to my life, and to our marriage in order to make them completely different from what our dysfunctional and painful pasts could have easily created. I like to call it a 'prescription' because God's way of doing relationships includes a lot of healing as well as a lot of health and great feelings!"

Heads nodded as this group of wounded travelers, Christians and non-Christians alike, waited to hear God's prescription for lasting relationships. What I shared with them, and with many others like them, I'd like to share with you, beginning in the next chapter.

Before we move on, however, I'd like you to evaluate your life and relational history. Take a few minutes to consider the questions below.

Personal Evaluation

1. What emotions were stirred within you as you read this chapter?

2. What former relationships came to mind that illustrated one or more of the points we covered? How do you feel about these relationships as you think about that era of your life?

3. To what extent does the Hollywood formula reflect how you've gone about doing relationships?

4. How successful has your approach been in developing and sustaining long-term, healthy relationships that include all areas of intimacy—the spiritual, emotional, and physical?

3

God's Prescription for Lasting Relationships

erhaps you're wondering, as some did in the divorce recovery group, whether these truths from the Bible apply to you. The people in the divorce recovery group needed to find hope that their lives and relationships could change and change for the better. I want to offer you the same hope. On the next page, next to the outline of the Hollywood formula, you will find the four components of God's prescription for lasting relationships which I shared with the group that night. Even though you may not initially understand the terms I am using, I want you to see the contrast in the approaches.

Don't worry for the moment if the comparisons are a little confusing. I still need to explain each of the steps in God's prescription, just as I did with Hollywood's scheme. Keeping these four steps in mind as we examine God's Word will help you track the differences between God's way of love and the world's pursuit of love.

God's prescription for relationships can be found throughout the Bible, but I think the following two verses summarize it well:

Therefore be imitators of God, as beloved children; and walk in love, just as Christ also loved you and gave Himself up for us, an offering and a sacrifice to God as a fragrant aroma.

Ephesians 5:1–2 NASB

As you read these verses, did any words or phrases obviously connect with components in God's prescription for relationships? Perhaps you noticed that these verses are the source for the phrase "walk in love." The other connections between these verses and the steps in God's prescription aren't quite as obvious, but I think you will see them as we continue.

Hollywood's Formula for Relationships	God's Prescription for Relationships
1. **Find** the right person.	1. **Become** the right person.
2. **Fall** in love.	2. **Walk** in love.
3. **Fix** your hopes and dreams on this person for your future fulfillment.	3. **Fix** your hope on God and seek to please him through this relationship.
4. If **failure** occurs, repeat steps 1, 2, and 3.	4. If **failure** occurs, repeat steps 1, 2, and 3.

The Context of God's Prescription

These two verses are a key statement of God's prescription in action, but in order to appreciate what they tell us, we need to know what comes before them. Ephesians is a book about how to live the miraculous new life in Christ. The first three chapters talk about what happens when the Spirit of God comes into a human being's heart, life, and soul. They describe what happens when we realize our need for God and turn to Christ. They explain how Christ's death made sufficient payment to settle our debt with God. They remind us that when the Spirit of God comes into us, we're redeemed and forgiven. Our past is put behind us.

These earlier chapters in Ephesians descril̶
pened in my life and in Theresa's life that c̶
and our approach to relationships. Ephes̶
divine prescription for the most personal c̶
God wants to bring into our lives. The first ha̶
Ephesians presents the basics about our relationshi̶

In this chapter we'll look at the parts of God's prescri̶
describe all the positive side effects that occur when God ̶
work in us. In the meantime, if the concepts above intrigue you, I'd
recommend that you read my book *Holy Transformation* (Moody
Press), which explains this process of radical change that God wants
to bring about in our lives.

In God's prescription for relationships, we begin with what he
does in our own lives. When God establishes a personal relationship
with us, his Spirit seals us and adopts us into a brand-new, Christ-
centered life. After teaching us about all that we receive in this new
life with Christ, the author of Ephesians
then describes how we are to relate to one
another in love. We are instructed to rely
on spiritual power we've never had before
as we speak, work, relate, and grow in our
love for God and our love for others.

> When God establishes a personal relationship with us, his Spirit seals us and adopts us into a brand-new, Christ-centered life.

The Four Steps in God's Prescription

To see the four steps in God's prescription for love, sex, and lasting relationships
as they are expressed here, look closely
again at the verses. Note that two clear commands outline the core
of loving others God's way. Below are the verses again with some
notations that I will explain during the course of this chapter.

[Therefore] <u>be imitators of God</u>, (as beloved children); and <u>walk
in love</u>, (just as Christ also loved you and gave Himself up for us),
{an offering} and {a sacrifice to God as a fragrant aroma}.

Ephesians 5:1–2 NASB

e underlined the phrases *be imitators of God* and *walk in* e because they are the commands. The word *be* indicates a ommand to become or show that you possess certain character traits. When it comes to God's prescription for the way you and I ought to live and love, there really isn't a question. God wants us to *be* a certain kind of people—his imitators. That's the first command in these two verses. And that brings us to step 1 of God's prescription for lasting relationships.

Step 1: Instead of looking for the right person, become the right person

The first command in Ephesians 5 tells us to be imitators of God by reflecting the way he loves us. Our love for others flows out of our sense of being deeply loved. Instead of constantly looking for the right person, God tells us to *become* the right person. Instead of looking for love, God tells us to realize that love has already found us! God loves as no one else ever can. The best way for us to demonstrate that we have understood and accepted God's love is to learn to imitate him as closely as possible in the way we treat others.

So, what does it look like to imitate God? The last verse of Ephesians 4 answers that question.

> Be kind and compassionate to one another, forgiving each other, just as in Christ God forgave you.
>
> Ephesians 4:32

In the Bible, terms like "therefore" or "but" are words that help ideas fit together and flow. They remind us to look at what was stated before. In Ephesians 5 it basically means, "In light of what has already been said, *therefore* be imitators and walk in love." It also means that the content of the verses that go before informs and controls the commands we are about to be given. Imitating God means that in relationships we are to be kind, tenderhearted, empathetic, discerning, willing to make allowance for people's mistakes, and consistently forgiving. It means we want good for them. We're gentle toward them even when our needs don't get met or when we're angry. That's when we go back to square one and forgive them. We let them off the hook. Why? Because we are superstars or spiritual giants? No, we forgive because we realize that we must pass on to others what God has given us. We who have been freely forgiven must, in turn, freely forgive. That's how we imitate God.

Now, once we identify the command *(be imitators of God)*, it's crucial to look for any further information about the command that we can find in the verses. What motivates us to imitate God is further emphasized and explained by the phrase, *as beloved children.* I put parentheses around those words, indicating that the phrase acts as a verb modifier. In other words, the way we practice imitating God will be affected or modified by our understanding that we are God's much-loved children.

You see, God loves you and me but not because of anything we've ever done. God cares for us, God delights in us, God is for us because that is his nature. As Romans 8:32 puts it, "He who did not spare his own Son, but gave him up for us all—how will he not also, along with him, graciously give us all things?" When the Bible speaks of love, it is describing an approach to others that has practically nothing to do with chemistry. God's Word never discounts feelings, but it clearly defines love as having much more to do with character and action than feelings. In other words, genuine love causes us to do things that have little or no good feelings necessarily attached to them. Ultimately, Jesus allowed himself to be nailed to a cross out of love for us, not because it felt good. We can spend a lifetime discovering the truth behind the simple thought in 1 John 4:19: "We love, because He first loved us" (NASB).

Our problem, however, is that loving isn't easy. You and I simply don't have the power to always forgive or be consistently kind. Our love, strength, will, and understanding don't stretch that far. We don't have the power to love this way unless we are so filled with God's love that we recognize that our deepest needs have already been met, and we're no longer expecting another human being to "complete" us.

It boils down to this. We will not be able to imitate God in our love for others unless we know that we are blessed, valuable, and significant—that we are loved. Our sense of being loved must not depend on this person liking us or that person coming through for us. You and I are not just "okay." In Christ, we are wonderful, significant, valuable, dearly loved, and the objects of God's infinite and unconditional affection. The God who made us and loves us tells us to live and love like he sees us and like he loves us. This is why the idea that having a great relationship is all about finding the right person is a lie. The key to developing a great relationship is *becoming* the right person.

> In Christ, we are wonderful, significant, valuable, dearly loved, and the objects of God's infinite and unconditional affection.

It's only when we grasp that God's love for us is boundless that we have the capacity to be genuine givers in a relationship. If we don't have that, what do we do? We try to get approval. We try to perform. We try to win affection. We attempt to manipulate in order to get what we want.

Les and Leslie Parrott illustrate this point brilliantly in their book *Relationships*. They teach a course at Seattle Pacific University called Relationships 101. It's an elective class, but the word is out on campus. Everyone signs up for the course. They tell the students on the first day, "This class is pass/fail. You don't have to take notes. But if you want to learn about relationships, here is one sentence we want you to write down. It will affect every relationship you have. However much you understand this sentence and apply it, all your relationships are transformed. But if you don't understand or are unwilling to do what this sentence says, your relationships will be dysfunctional." Having achieved the undivided attention of 250 college students, they make the following statement: **"If you attempt to build intimacy with a person before you've done the hard work of becoming a whole and healthy person, every relationship will be an attempt to**

complete the hole in your heart and the lack of what you don't have. That relationship will end in disaster."[1]

Allow me to paraphrase the Parrotts' statement. Any time you want to build intimacy with a person before your identity is fully in Christ and you know and feel secure and strong in him, you will be expecting that person to do something for you that he or she cannot do. In other words, when your identity is in Christ, you don't need others the same way, you don't have to perform, and they don't have to come through in order for your ultimate needs to be met.

The world says, "Set your hope on this person to come through for you. Make this person the center of your existence." It doesn't work. The problem is, that person is weak, imperfect, and needy, just like you and just like me. That person is going to blow it, right? It hurts, so what do we do? We retaliate, or we manipulate, or we blame. Because the world teaches us to expect from others what God alone can give us, we are unable to appreciate the very real (though limited) wonders of human love.

The key to lasting relationships is developing a relationship with God through Christ in such a way that you are secure in who you are in him. That allows you to be a giver and a real lover. If you do not get there (and there is some hard work involved to understand your identity in Christ, by the way), all your relationships will be handicapped. How do you get there? The first three chapters of Ephesians spell out the process. Until you establish an unshakable identity in Christ, every relationship will be an attempt to get something from that person to make you feel like you're okay. Some of us will manipulate, some of us will get overly attached and dependent, but all of us will produce dysfunctional relationships.

Step 2: Instead of falling in love, walk *in love*

If you refer again to Ephesians 5:1–2, you will see I added parentheses around the phrase, *just as Christ also loved you and gave Himself up for us*. This phrase explains how the command to *walk in love* works. *Walk in love* means something much deeper than taking long strolls on the beach or wandering hand-in-hand through the mall. In fact, walking in love means that we love others *in exactly the same way that Christ loved us*. How did Christ love us? The phrase supplies the answer: *He gave himself up for you*. So, here's the deeper application: Walking in love is about sacrificial commitment.

The following definition of what it means to walk in love helps me personally and is the key to my relationship with Theresa: Walking in love means giving the other person what he or she needs the most when it is least deserved, because that's exactly how God has treated you. That's what genuine love is. Love is giving the other person in the relationship what he or she needs the most, not necessarily what he or she wants the most. There are many times in my marriage, with my kids, and in great friendships that, by the grace of God, I've given people what they needed, but not necessarily what they wanted. And when I gave them what they really needed, they got angry. I gave my kids correction and they didn't like it at the time. I told friends the truth when they hoped I would agree with a lie they believed, and they got upset with me. I've been honest with Theresa at times when being dishonest might avoid an argument, and that's created some uncomfortable moments.

> The love that walks is an other-centered love.

Please realize that the principle cuts both ways. There are people who have given me what I needed instead of what I wanted and I've gotten really mad at them. I had my mind made up about decisions as varied as what car or house to buy, or how to advise our kids about college choices. Then Theresa asked the one question I didn't want to hear but needed to consider. I didn't like that. I've made some decisions about the direction of our church that were hasty, and those decisions got questioned by people who I know care for me. And even though part of me knew they asked their questions out of their love for me, I didn't enjoy being challenged. I got hurt and there was some shame over the disappointment. Life in those moments wasn't Hollywood at all. And then I grew up some. Now I know they were meeting my real needs while I wanted them to meet my felt needs.

Love is a sacrificial, other-centered action that provides what's best for the other person. God's way is very hard on the feelings, but it's very healthy for the soul. It works wonders in relationships where both parties find their ultimate identity in Christ.

That's why the second step in God's plan for relationships involves genuine love. Don't *fall* in love, God tells us, *walk* in love. Genuine love isn't a passive, quivering mass of good feelings; genuine love is a deliberate, intentional, honest, and even painful giving up of self-preservation for another person's good. The love that walks is an other-centered love. It says, "I'm going to give you what you need," and then follows through. No manipulation, no games, and no power play. And, interestingly enough, it's when we love in this way that we actually fan the flames of romance and those good feelings we all long to enjoy. As we consciously take these first two steps in God's plan, they lead us directly to step 3.

Step 3: Instead of fixing your hopes and dreams on another person, fix your hope on God *and seek to please him through this relationship*

When it comes to marriage, as we have said, the Hollywood formula is tragically wrong. In the Hollywood version of a wedding ceremony, the couple stands face to face before their gathered friends. These ceremonies are often filmed in sets that look like places of worship, though there is rarely any real recognition of God in the event. The couple basically declares, "You are the most important person in my life. You complete me. You are my perfect mate, the answer to all my dreams."

In a wedding that honors God's presence and role, the two people also face each other, welcoming God's blessing and fully acknowledging that they expect God to help them keep the promises they make. But their view of one another could be expressed this way, "You are *not* the most important person in my life—Christ is. And because Christ is the most important person in my life, I'm going to treat you even better than I could treat you if you were the most important person in my life. Christ will help me love you more than I could ever love you in my own strength alone."

In our Bible verses I bracketed the phrases *an offering* and *a sacrifice* because these two little phrases have to do with serving and selfless devotion. Jesus didn't do something primarily because it would please us; he did something that was pleasing to God. I know what I'm about to say sounds heretical, but the goal of relationships is not to make sure everything goes our way or makes us happy. The goal is to please God. The best the world can offer as a model for marriage involves two people who are trying hard to please each other. God's prescription creates an exciting prospect in which two people are actually learning to please a third—God—by the way they respond to him and to each other.

> God's prescription creates an exciting prospect in which two people are actually learning to please a third— God—by the way they respond to him and to each other.

I want to make this point very clear. When we go the other route and make our personal fulfillment the goal of every relationship, it never works out. And then we wrongly assume the problem is the other person, so we go and find someone else. We see extreme forms of this behavior played out on prime-time television in many of the so-called reality shows. Bachelors or bachelorettes in highly artificial settings put a dozen or more people to the test. How far will the contestants go to gain the attention of the central figure, who passes out roses or jewelry to those who "make the grade." What a place to be, we think, having a whole crowd vie for our favor. But it isn't reality. And the promised fairy-tale endings always fade into darkness. Those shows reveal and tease our selfish wishes. How do we break this ingrained self-centered cycle in our lives? How do we address these narcissistic desires and our personal need to be center stage? How do we stop expecting the world to revolve around us?

The answer involves a completely different approach. Instead of trying to find out what's wrong with the other person, instead of continually expecting him or her to conform to our needs, we must ask God to make us who he wants us to be and to help us to walk in love, giving sacrificially what the other person needs. In my case, it means I can't fix my hope on whether or not my wife is being affectionate. It means accepting that everything is not going to work out great or just the way I want it to all the time. There are times when life is really hard and not filled with good feelings at all. You and I need to be willing to endure the pain and go through the tough times. You see, as long as we live with this deluded idea that sets the other person up to meet all our expectations, we are doomed to disappointment. Great relationships involve struggle, conflict, working through issues, and refusing to demand, consciously or not, that the other person make our lives work. The result is a lot of personal growth and relational health.

God is inviting you into a life of thoughtful, sacrificial love in your relationships. It will be the most challenging pursuit you have ever undertaken. But let me add this good news. The by-product of God's approach to relationships is the very kind of intimacy, love, sex, and lasting companionship you and I have always wanted.

Lest we end up thinking we've got a simple, connect-the-dots, create-a-miracle plan, we need to understand that God's prescription for relationships, just like the inferior Hollywood formula, also has a fourth step. Why? Because God understands us perfectly.

Step 4: If failure occurs, repeat steps 1, 2, and 3

Interestingly enough, the fourth step in both the Hollywood formula and in God's prescription are identical but for radically different reasons. Both steps recognize an inevitable feature of human relationships—failure. Even if we are utterly convinced of the truth of God's way, do you think we can follow these steps flawlessly from this day forward? Of course not. When it comes to failure in a relationship, the real question isn't *if*, but *when*.

If you're married, the person who might fail isn't necessarily your mate. If you're a man, the person you're looking at in the mirror while you are shaving is a prime candidate. If you're a woman, the face you see in your makeup mirror may belong to the person who fails. There may be times when you will think, "I feel like this relationship is hopeless. I'm disillusioned. I'm really struggling." God's prescription doesn't say you can't have those feelings from time to time. But it simply won't allow you to conclude, "Well, maybe I've got the wrong person." If those little doubts aren't challenged and crushed, they start to undermine your commitment. Then, when you get treated a little better by someone else, you're tempted to jump to comparative conclusions, "Wow, he or she sure treats me better than my spouse!" And you begin to think she's kind of cute or he really understands you—not at all like your wife or husband. And the Hollywood formula clicks in. You don't even realize it. Suddenly, you're on the lookout for someone new. Is this a good plan and a good path? No. All you'll do is wreck two homes, scar a bunch of kids for life, have all kinds of problems, and end up with more baggage than before. Those may sound like extreme results, but they are all too familiar to a large segment of our society today.

This sequence of events doesn't have to be your experience or the end of the line for you. Instead, you can crush those little lies while they are little. You can look in the mirror when you're putting on your makeup or shaving cream and say, "Hmm, we have a problem in this relationship and I'm not very fulfilled right now. In fact, I'm downright angry and she is too. And that couch is really hard to sleep on. Now, am I the man or woman you want me to be, Lord Jesus? Am I walking in love? What would you want to do in me, whether my mate changes at all, to imitate you and walk in love so this relationship can be pleasing to you?"

Do you see what a radically different approach this is? Do you see how looking in the mirror shifts your focus off your natural tendency to blame your partner and on to what you can do about making things better? The truth of the matter is that blaming or trying to get our mates to change is usually counterproductive anyway. But by contrast, how much control do we have over changing the person in the mirror? One hundred percent. How much responsibility do we bear for our actions and choices? One hundred percent. How much do our relationships gain when we try to manipulate our mates, or try to make them into some other kind of person? Not very much. This becomes one of those moments when we calmly and honestly face a failure. Step 4 of the prescription takes over. **God tells us to start over on step 1—choose to become the right person.** We should make that our focus. We walk through the steps: imitate God, walk in love, fix our hope on God, and seek to please him in every one of our relationships. If failure occurs (and it will), we go back to square one and take the steps again.

You may be thinking, "I've got to get my own relationship with God in order before I can even begin to address the mess in my life." Find someone who can help you with that. Over and over I have heard people say, wistfully, "I wish I had known about God's prescription twenty years ago." Others have said, "I've got kids who need to understand this. They think they're going to do love better than I have, but now I know they're following the same dead-end scheme. I want to tell them they really can do better than I did, but they'll have to do it differently!" Although Theresa and I don't particularly enjoy reviewing some very difficult events in our past, when we see that people benefit from being able to understand why so much of our culture has detoured into a wilderness of shattered relationships and broken hearts, revisiting the pain in our lives is worthwhile.

My years of teaching divorce recovery workshops exposed me to hundreds of people in relational crises of every sort. I've concluded from those who have suffered the most that the Hollywood formula seems to have a stranglehold on our culture. If I wasn't convinced that God's prescription will be true no matter what happens to our culture, I'd be tempted to give up. But when I see my own children living out this prescription, flourishing in their marriages and lives, I know I'm participating in something worthwhile. Hundreds of marriages have been saved by being built or rebuilt using God's prescription, which brings us back to this book and the reason why I'm sharing this message with you. I trust you see the radical differences between the Hollywood formula and God's prescription for relationships as they relate to your life. Recognizing those differences will help you avoid many of the mistakes being made by people all around you.

A Few Words of Caution

I know that the people who will read these pages will in many ways parallel the audiences in our divorce recovery program. What we've seen and heard in our sessions simply reflects the wider culture. The divorce rate between Christians and unbelievers is about the same. How could this be? Because we've all been shaped by our culture. We've been seduced, hoodwinked, and manipulated by a steady diet of the Hollywood formula.

Even in the evangelical church, average Christians who really do know God and are in the faith often live by the world's code. We unconsciously go about relationships Hollywood's way. We go about finances Wall Street's way. And we approach parenting with whatever techniques we think will work or happen to be the current childrearing fad. We have so segmented and compartmentalized our lives that our behavior reflects that we listen more to the world than to God's Word. We've exchanged God's prescription for Hollywood's formula with disastrous and painful results. No wonder the divorce rate is about the same between believers and unbelievers.

These are not the only statistics worth considering, however. In places where God's prescription is being taught and among families where God's prescription is being practiced, we see remarkable results! Among those couples who attend church regularly (not just once a month), who pray together regularly, and who each have personal devotional time with God, the divorce rate is in the low single digits. Why? Because they're following God's divine design. Do they have struggles? Absolutely. But do you know what they do? They imitate God, they forgive, they are kind, they look at their hearts, and they sacrificially put each other's needs before their own. They do that for a year, then five, and then ten. Then they may go through seasons with pressures, kids, and finances, but God does a great work and helps them pull through. It's very hard and very good. The reward, legacy, and blessing add up to intimacy and joy with each other. Not ooey-gooey electric feelings every day. In fact, some days are downright dreary. It's a fallen world and they're married to another fellow struggler just like them. They know that they need constant forgiveness, and they give and receive it.

In those marriages established on God's prescription, children are secure, safe, and confident. Spouses who practice imitating God in their relationship with each other do the same with their kids. They develop an awesome family relationship in spite of all the normal struggles and challenges. The exciting thing is that the kids get to see what real relationships look like as they watch their parents. They pick up that torch and become the right people in their own marriages, continually walking and occasionally failing as they follow God's prescription. If that sounds like wistful thinking or spiritual platitudes, think again. I just described what the last twenty-five years of living has been like for Theresa and me, and what I now see in our grown children. We've come out of dysfunctional pasts and made lots of mistakes, but a deep, intimate, exciting, and still very romantic relationship has been God's reward.

Conclusion

God wants that for you. You don't have to be a tragic statistic. You don't have to be afraid to make a commitment. There is a supernatural way to do relationships. God will use it in your life and you'll leave behind a legacy.

As believers, we have to do relationships God's way. The price tag is too high and it breaks God's heart way too often when we do relationships Hollywood's way. The side-by-side comparisons ought to be burned into our consciences. We must develop a sensitivity that alerts us to situations in which the Hollywood formula seeks to click in to our thinking. The better we understand and practice God's prescription for love, sex, and lasting relationships, the more we will see through the lies and ultimate disappointment of any alternative.

I know there are still many questions—probably more than when you started this book. What to do about those feelings and strange attractions represents a huge area of difficulty in many people's lives. That's the territory we'll explore in the next chapter.

Personal Evaluation

1. The first step in God's prescription for love, sex, and lasting relationships involves a shift from trying to find the right person to becoming the right person. How would you explain that to someone who hadn't read the book yet?

2. What is the difference between "falling in love" and "walking in love"?

3. When it comes to a relationship with another person, what does it mean to "fix your hope on God" rather than on the other person?

4. What do you find most compelling or intriguing about God's prescription for love, sex, and lasting relationships?

5. What specific action step would you need to take in order to begin following God's prescription for relating to the opposite sex?

4

Before You "Fall in Love"

Falling in love is tricky business. But we don't let that stop us. In fact, from ancient times until now, the phenomenon we call "falling in love" has been one of the most sought after experiences by the human species. We want to trip and plunge into that tumbling, bottomless, breathless pit of overwhelming attraction. We welcome this state of emotional euphoria even though it often results in some of the poorest, most regrettable, and most painful choices of our lives. Yes, falling in love is tricky business.

The ancient Greeks had an interesting take on falling in love; they compared it to going insane. Most of us who have "fallen in love" know the Greeks had a point. As we are drawn into relationship with the opposite sex, it seems that the attraction is controlled by some unknown and mysterious power that overrides our reason and produces unexplainable but undeniable emotions. And we like those feelings. They're intoxicating and irresistible.

American author Marilyn French captures the essence of "falling in love" when she writes, "It is the taking over of a rational and lucid mind by delusion and self-destruction. You lose yourself, you have no power over yourself, and you can't even think straight." She's describing an odd state but true and familiar to all of us. "Falling in love" produces some of the most wonderful and powerful emotions we can experience, while simultaneously warping our ability to think clearly.

We were made to love and be loved.

The German philosopher Nietzsche went so far as to say, "Love is the state in which man sees things most widely different from what they are." Current research would tend to support Nietzsche's observation. Relational experts Les and Leslie Parrott conclude the following after interviewing and counseling thousands of couples. "Indeed, steamy starts do not promote our best thinking. Intense emotions often block us from taking a careful and objective look at ourselves, the person we are dating, and the relationship we are forming together."[1] Whether we scan across the centuries or simply read the latest research, one thing becomes abundantly clear—"falling in love" is indeed tricky business.

Despite all its apparent dangers and drawbacks, this desire to "fall in love" remains one of our most passionate pursuits. We were made to love and be loved. But why is this process of connecting with the opposite sex complicated by so many relational risks? How can something so natural and beautiful lead us into such unhealthy relationships filled with pain, disappointment, and dysfunction? Why is falling in love such tricky business, and what do we need to know in order to navigate successfully through this wonderful yet dangerous voyage of emotions?

What You Can't Afford Not to Know

I'd like to suggest there are a couple of answers to the questions above. The first answer has to do with our lack of perspective concerning the whole concept of love. Our inability to clearly define love itself makes knowing when you're actually "in love" next to impossible. As long as love remains a foggy, fuzzy mystery somewhere out there that you only know by supercharged emotional surges, you'll always be adrift in an ocean of uncertainty rather than sailing to solid land. Until you are crystal clear on what it really means to love another person, you'll never be sure if what you are experiencing is real or just something like a hallucination or a fleeting feeling.

A second answer deals with the widespread confusion over the difference between love and infatuation. Feelings are like fire—they were made to burn, not to worry about where they are burning. When the relational sparks start to fly, there's little immediate indication whether what's about to happen is a destructive explosion, an emotional dud, or the flare-up of a fire that will warm a relationship for decades to come.

Interestingly, there has been significant research done with people experiencing what we call infatuation. When we have this experience we could call falling into infatuation (or falling into romantic interest), chemicals are secreted in the brain, causing light-headedness, dizziness, and a flood of emotions that we can't explain. Certain people trigger that kind of response in us. We are almost instantly drawn to them. Unfortunately, this unexpected, internal condition has often been called "falling in love." This reaction to attraction, which we could also describe as a "chemically induced crush," is actually infatuation. Who among us has not walked into a room, made eye contact with a complete stranger, and felt an instant, unexpected rush of emotion and attraction? Who hasn't had that sudden impulse to look again?

Why these moments happen and what exactly triggers them—who knows? But the feelings are definitely a temporary condition. The attraction is neither irresistible nor dependable. You can easily experience infatuation with people who would turn out to be relational nightmares. That's why it is so dangerous to use infatuation as a sign to pursue a relationship. If you and I don't know the difference between infatuation and love, we are destined to make some of the dumbest and most regrettable decisions we'll ever make. These bad decisions come with heavy and painful price tags.

So you see, it's imperative in this tricky business of "falling in love" that we take the time to clearly define what we mean by the word "love." The investment will pay off handsomely. We can actually learn how to avoid future relational baggage and how to recognize authentic love relationships when we clarify two crucial issues: (1) what love is, and (2) what the difference is between love and infatuation.

What Love Is

In English the word *love* can refer to just about anything. That's the problem. I can look into the eyes of my wife and in a moment of truth-telling say, "Theresa, I love you." Hours later, a good friend can come over to my house and say, "I love running marathons." (Frankly, I find it difficult to understand how anyone can love running 26.2 miles without stopping.) How can the word I use for my deepest feelings toward my wife be the same word my friend uses to express his enjoyment of a sport? Then my daughter responds to my suggestion that we eat out by saying, "Oh Dad, I don't want to go to that restaurant. I'd really love some pizza!" When we practice the habit of ending the sentence "I love _____" in a thousand relatively insignificant ways, we import so many meanings into the word *love* that it ceases to mean much of anything. It becomes little more than a foggy and unclear notion associated with positive feelings. We use it to express almost any desire or attraction, no matter how trivial. Can you see how such a vague and uncertain definition of love leaves us groping for words when we are trying to discern what to do in the most important relationships in our lives? Frankly, we need help.

Three Kinds of Love

The Greek language is much more precise than English in describing relationships. It uses three words that can be translated into English as "love." From these words we derive the three major types of love that we need to consider when we say "I love you" to someone.

Eros Love—The Love of Sexual Passion

The first Greek term for love is *eros*. English actually borrowed this foreign word to create one of our own—"erotic." The Greeks used the word *eros* to refer to a need-centered love or desire based on attraction and fulfillment. *Eros* is characterized by passion and sexual desire. *Eros* describes the aspect of a relationship between a man and a woman that is most like magnetism. Magnets aren't choosy. Their drawing capacity remains "on" continuously, instantly attracted to any object that has the right characteristics. Men and women created by God have, as part of their design, a capacity for attraction that is neither under their complete control nor capable of entirely controlling them against their will. This *eros* aspect of love is God-given and necessary for marriages to succeed; however, marriage cannot be sustained by *eros* alone. It's a part of God's plan, but not all of it.

For some of you, the last paragraph may have felt like we just crossed a dangerous line in having the words "God" and "erotic" in the same sentence. Unfortunately, Christians have a reputation for believing that God is uncomfortable when it comes to sex and that the Bible is definitely against it. But no, God invented erotic love. Like it or not, you and I are living proof that sex works. The Bible never treats sex itself as something other than a natural and beautiful part of God's design, just as capable of being dirtied and shamed by sin as the rest of God's creation. But the emphasis on sex in the Scriptures is far from negative.

> The Bible never treats sex itself as something other than a natural and beautiful part of God's design

Although there are passages in Scripture that clearly deserve an R rating—for example, most of Song of Solomon—the protections that God places around sex aren't there because something is wrong with sex. They are in place because something is wrong with us. Sex is a sacred and private part of a marriage relationship. Far from being dirty in any way or a "necessary evil," as some misguided theologians of the past have termed it, erotic love in marriage is blessed and encouraged by God. He even calls it holy.

Sexual union offers a couple one of the most powerful ways to experience the oneness that the Bible refers to when it describes marriage (see Genesis 2:24–25).

In fact, many biblical passages offer explicit instructions regarding the sanctity of sex in marriage. In Proverbs, chapter 5, a wise father instructs his son:

> Drink water from your own cistern,
>> running water from your own well.
> Should your springs overflow in the streets,
>> your streams of water in the public squares?
> Let them be yours alone,
>> never to be shared with strangers.
> May your fountain be blessed,
>> and may you rejoice in the wife of your youth.
> A loving doe, a graceful deer—
>> may her breasts satisfy you always,
>> may you ever be captivated [literally, *intoxicated*] by her love.
>
> Proverbs 5:15–19

What a vivid, healthy, and delightful description of marital sexuality! God is not a prude. God created sexual attraction and erotic love as a fundamental part of relationships between men and women. Unfortunately, Hollywood has made *eros* all there is to love. Erotic love is the fire and the passion. Well, it's true that *eros* is fire, passion, and a wonderful part of marital love. But there's much more to love than the sparks and fire of *eros*. Fire is fantastic in the right place, at the right time. When it is in the fireplace, it warms and cheers a room. It adds a special and wonderful ambience to it. But if you pull the flaming logs out of the fireplace and put them on the floor of the house, the entire structure will soon go up in smoke and ash. Today we're living in a culture where people have so focused on the *eros* aspect of love that the power and wonder of sexual intimacy has been lost. Casual sex, "hooking up," and love according to hormones have left countless people empty and longing for genuine love and lasting connection.

God designed the *eros* part of love for delightful and specific purposes. In the fireplace of the marital relationship, let *eros* burn, baby, let it burn. But to think that *eros* love can sustain a relationship is both naïve and shortsighted. In fact, it is the other aspects of love in a relationship that, in unique ways, stoke the fires in the fireplace.

PHILEO LOVE—THE LOVE OF BEST FRIENDS

The Greeks called the second kind of love *phileo*. This is friendship love. The Bible uses the word "companionship" several times to describe this part of a marriage relationship. *Phileo* love means reciprocal sharing of time, hobbies, activities, home, games, and other aspects of fellowship. One English word that applies the Greek term *phileo* is our word "Philadelphia," the city of brotherly love.

Phileo refers to that mutuality, that friendship part of love. *Eros* looks at a man and a woman as lovers. *Phileo* looks at a man and a woman as best friends. One New Testament passage that expands our understanding of *phileo* is Romans 12:9–13.

> Love must be sincere. Hate what is evil; cling to what is good. Be devoted to one another in brotherly love. Honor one another above yourselves. Never be lacking in zeal, but keep your spiritual fervor, serving the Lord. Be joyful in hope, patient in affliction, faithful in prayer. Share with God's people who are in need. Practice hospitality.

Please take a moment and read that passage again, but this time notice the tone of the words and attitudes. Do you sense Paul's desire to build communion and commitment that affect every part of our lives and relationships? Can you feel the health and winsomeness that exude from every phrase? Wouldn't it be great if this passage described how you were treated by the love of your life?

The Greek word for *love* in the first sentence is actually the third type of love we will examine below. But the qualities of sincerity, hatred towards evil, and hanging on ***"to what is good"*** anticipate the outline of *phileo* (brotherly love) that begins in verse 10. The highlighted qualities of love are authenticity and genuineness. Then come the practical, everyday aspects of relationship—***"Be devoted to one another in brotherly love (phileo)."*** Our relationships, in order to be healthy and lasting, should be characterized by devotion and commitment. Well, what does that look like? First, ***"Honor one another above yourselves."*** In other words, view those around you as worthy of attention, encouragement, respect, and admiration. ***"Never be lacking in zeal, but keep your spiritual fervor, serving the Lord."*** Our motivation for the way we treat each other always comes back, not to their ultimate worthiness, but to our relationship with Christ. The way we love others is an expression of our heartfelt and grateful service to Christ.

> The way we love others is an expression of our heartfelt and grateful service to Christ.

The description of *phileo* continues with, ***"Be joyful in hope, patient in affliction, faithful in prayer. Share with God's people who are in need."***

Each of these phrases states a "quick comparative" that begins with a challenge to a certain standard of response (joy, patience, faithfulness, sharing) followed immediately by an arena of action (hope, affliction, prayer, need). In other words, joyfulness is not a giddy ignorance or denial of hardships in life; rather it is a conscious, hopeful outlook that always remembers that God is in control. Patience doesn't really come into its own until there is affliction. Faithfulness to someone in brotherly love actually has a lot to do with how we pray for one another. And sharing means more when we've taken time to observe what others need and have done what we could to meet those needs.

The apostle Paul ends this passage with a pithy command, ***"Practice hospitality."*** In the ancient world hospitality always involved providing food and shelter to those in need. But notice that when we love with *phileo* love, we are to "practice" it in the same way that a doctor practices medicine. When we practice hospitality, we get better at it. This command means doing life in such a way that you put the practical needs of other people first. In our day, this may mean moving beyond simply giving food and shelter to taking time to meet the emotional needs of your mate. It may mean going to the mall, the grocery store, or taking a long walk when you don't want to. In marriage, practicing hospitality can mean something as obvious as fixing things around the house.

Phileo love involves doing life as friends, with loyalty and communication. It's about sitting down, when you don't feel like it, and going over the budget and making decisions. It's speaking the truth in love when you've been irritated or wounded. *Phileo* love faces the hard issues and willingly keeps them on the table, always gently seeking forgiveness and restoration from the heart.

If *eros* love is the spark that repeatedly ignites our passion, then *phileo* love is the steady fuel that feeds our joy. Doing life together, not only as passionate lovers but as best friends, is at the core of genuine love, satisfying sex, and a lasting relationship. And although we almost instinctively know that's the kind of life we want, our efforts fall short. We humans often display rapidly fluctuating feelings and inconsistent affection. Our capacity for *eros* and *phileo* love can flare and then fade, like flames without enough air or firewood. As much as *eros* and *phileo* contribute to a healthy relationship, they need help. They need a third companion to bring depth, strength, and lasting character to romance and friendship. That's why the most influential kind of love we can experience and express is sacrificial love—*agape* love.

Agape Love—The Love of Sacrificial Commitment

The third kind of love captured in the Greek language is called *agape* love. This is giving love. It acts unilaterally, meaning this love reaches out even if the person being loved doesn't recognize the love. *Agape* love gives even when the partner doesn't respond as hoped. It's giving and meeting the real needs of another and helping that person to become a better, more mature individual. It is selfless love.

Agape love takes the initiative and energizes the other two kinds of love. The classic biblical passage that outlines this kind of love, unfortunately, has been trivialized. Instead of being lived out by us as believers, it is found mostly on little plaques hung in bathrooms. It gets printed on wedding program covers but is seldom understood by the couple. The words are so familiar that we are likely to hear them without letting their meaning penetrate our minds. This time, as you read them, think what would happen in a relationship between a man and a woman if what you are about to read described how they actually treated each other in the ups and downs of daily life.

> Love is patient,
> love is kind.
> It does not envy,
> it does not boast,
> it is not proud.
> It is not rude,
> it is not self-seeking,
> it is not easily angered,
> it keeps no record of wrongs.
> Love does not delight in evil
> but rejoices with the truth.
> It always protects,
> always trusts,
> always hopes,
> always perseveres.
> Love never fails.

1 Corinthians 13:4–8a

Phileo love is a friendship love that requires a high level of mutuality—we give, expecting something in return. But *agape* love is when you give, not because your mate has done something nice or because he or she is wonderful all the time, but even at times when your mate has wounded you. This is the kind of love that we're told to exhibit in Ephesians 4:32, when it says, **"Be kind to one another, tenderhearted, forgiving one another, even as God in Christ forgave you"** (NKJV). This is exactly the kind of love the apostle Paul has in mind when he begins Ephesians 5 by urging us to *"walk in love"*—to live out an *agape* love.

This *agape* love is a God-given, supernatural, and unconditional love. The 1 Corinthians 13 passage says that, first of all, love is *"patient."* We could stop right there. Patience means putting up with a lot of junk over a long period of time and not retaliating. Next, the passage says *"love is kind,"* which means that it not only looks for positive ways to express concern and meet needs but also lacks any hint of envy, jealousy, boasting, pride, rudeness, self-seeking, quick temper, recorded offenses, or delighting in evil.

In *agape* love, the relationship is not about you. It's not about your life or about what you can get. It's about how you can serve the other person. When you love this way, you're not easily angered. You don't blow up. You don't pout. You don't give up and take your ball and go home. Unlike Hollywood's version of love that depends on passionate feelings, good looks, and pleasant circumstances, this kind of love remains loyal and steadfast even in the worst of times.

> *Agape* love is giving others what they *need* most when they *deserve* it the least.

Agape love *"keeps no record of wrongs."* It makes allowances for others' shortcomings and mistakes, like we want them to make for us when we fail. *"Love does not delight in evil but rejoices with the truth"*—not "See, I caught you" but "You know what? You're busted and I love you. How can we work this out?" It's the kind of love that looks past the other's failure, that believes in them when they don't even believe in themselves. It's a God-given, other-centered commitment to our partner that *"always protects, always trusts, always hopes, and always perseveres."* This is the kind of love that is so powerful that it *"never fails."* It says, "No matter what, I'm with you." That's what *agape* love is—the love that keeps on giving and giving.

Eros love has to do with heightened emotions and raw attraction. *Phileo* love has to do with friendship, communion, and sharing. *Agape* love has to do with unconditional loyalty and sacrificial commitment. In fact, *agape* love can be summed up best by the following statement: It's giving others what they need most when they deserve it the least.

If you thought to yourself after you read that summary, *That sounds impossible,* you're right! *Agape* love *is* impossible! *Agape* love cannot be manufactured by human effort or willpower, and yet it is absolutely essential for deep love, intimate sex, and a lasting relationship. Now, if it seems a bit confusing to insist we need to have a kind of love that's impossible to create on our own, then let me explain a little theory I have about how relationships work.

Ingram's Theory of Relationships

I have a theory. It isn't in the Bible per se; it's just a theory. It might not be exactly how life works, but it makes a lot of sense to me. I think God played a cosmic trick on us. The trick is that he placed in my heart and yours this unbelievable drive and passion for intimacy and relationships. Then he created relationships. He made men and women with different needs, such that each partner would also need a supernatural power source to forgive, love, care, and do for the other even when they didn't feel like it, just as God has done for us. In this way, God would constantly make us aware of our need for him as we seek to find love and fulfillment in relationships. In God's ingenious design, a couple would resist the temptation to believe that they didn't need God because they had each other; rather, they would come to know that they needed God's participation if they were going to keep each other. Without that acknowledgment of God's involvement, the relationship can easily fall apart.

If you're not quite tracking with me on this theory of relationships, let me visualize it this way. Let's return to our earlier two models of relationship and add a few features that will help you see how God designed relationships to work with him at the center.

Leaving God, the source of *agape* love, out of a relationship sets it up for failure. If you do that, you'll go through lots of relation-

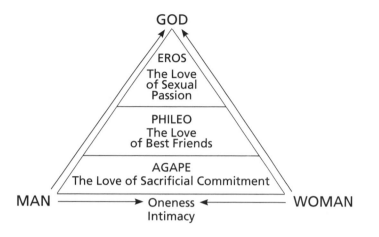

ships, wound others, wound yourself, become very discouraged, eventually assume there is something wrong with you, and experience a host of personal and relational problems. Does that sound like many of the relationships you have observed or experienced? Does that sound like a pattern you've noticed in people's lives, including your own? You see, if you seriously desire to have a great relationship that goes beyond just wanting to get your needs met or playing the game "I'll love you if you love me," then you will have to break the pattern. You will have to establish your relationship on a spiritual foundation. If you ever want to love radically and experience intimacy as God intended, you'll come to the point where you'll realize, "**I can't do this!** I can't make this relationship work. I've tried all this communication stuff and counseling—but it's beyond my strength to love this person when he treats me in ways that hurt my feelings." Oh, you might do it for a few weeks if you're determined, but I believe God has designed relationships in such a way that your deepest longings will be frustrated until you realize that you need supernatural power to love the most important person in your life.

Remember our earlier triangular picture of God's design—he's at the top. A man and woman, with all their passion for intimacy, start at the bottom corners of the pyramid. And the closer each of these partners gets to God, what happens? The relational distance between the man and woman become smaller. Intimacy gets closer.

If you are ever going to know for sure if you're in love, you have to look at love beyond the Hollywood formula—affection, meet someone, try to work it out, get the strong feelings. You need to define love clearly. What better way to define love than according to the One who is love and who originally loved us?

Love is a cord of three strands woven together in balance and timing. The cord includes passionate *eros*, friendly *phileo*, and giving *agape*. According to Ephesians 5:1–2, our ultimate objective in love is to treat others the way God has treated us. Each kind of love makes a particular contribution to a healthy relationship, particularly marriage.

How to Improve Your Love Life

You are beginning to understand a completely new paradigm of what it means to be in love. So where do you go from here? You and I have spent most of our waking hours being told that love merely has to do with feelings, passion, chance meetings, and chemistry. But we all know that relationships based on those fleeting elements alone produce the kind of chaos and tragedy that we see all around us. It doesn't have to be that way. With a proper understanding of what it means to love and be loved, you can begin doing relationships differently. God loves you and wants you to learn how to share your life in a significant way with a person of the opposite sex. Let's review the steps to help you move toward deep, loving relationships.

> Step 1 Define love. It's not just feelings; it's *eros*, *phileo*, and *agape*.
>
> Step 2 Discern between infatuation and love.

In the next chapter we'll look at twelve specific questions that will help this discerning process. For now, begin to note the difference. When it comes to heightened infatuation, you may find you are prone to "fall in love" every day. That's not the kind of love that builds toward a lasting relationship. Infatuation is easy come/easy go; genuine love is for keeps—it lasts.

I can't wait for you to read the next chapter as we learn together how to tell the difference between infatuation and real love. I've been repeatedly told that the information in the next chapter is some of the most helpful in the entire book. But before we go there, let me provide you with some immediate practical help in improving your love life.

A Word to Singles

Keep your emotional and physical involvement behind your leading from God and your commitment to the other person.

If you are a single or a newly single person, let me encourage you to delay physical involvement in any new relationships. Early and escalating physical contacts in the first phases of a relationship affect your thinking and set you up for failure. This axiom—keep your emotional and physical involvement behind your leading from God and commitment to the other person—will serve you well. It will guard you from dysfunctional relationships. It will allow the *eros* aspect of the relationship to come in at the right time and in good ways. Instead of experiencing guilt, shame, and another cycle of breakup, you will learn to do relationships in a new and healthy way. Later on, we will talk much more about how to build a spiritual foundation, and how to move from that starting point toward observing the inner circle and character of the person with whom you are developing a new relationship. God has a lot to teach us about each step of growing into love—social, psychological, emotional, and physical. Increasing levels of intimacy will develop naturally, rather than being balanced precariously on a tiny point of emotions and first impressions.

A Word to the Married

Healthy love requires the involvement of all three types of love. Examine each one, determine which one your mate needs most, and choose to give it as an act of worship to God.

This axiom for married folks isn't hard to figure out—it's just hard to practice. The complaints I hear from couples are so predictable, they would be funny if they didn't create such heartache and trouble. Husbands tend to say, "There's not enough *eros* in our marriage!" Wives immediately respond, "There's not enough *phileo* in our marriage!" That's the classic stalemate we have to get beyond. These are legitimate needs—but the wrong starting point. If you really want to improve your marriage, it's always safe to begin the process of change by assuming that your partner needs *agape* love from you. Not because he or she deserves it or because it's top on your list. You make this decision because you have experienced Christ's love and realize that meeting someone else's need is the best way to express how grateful you are for Christ's love. This means that a wife chooses to treat her husband in ways that are meaningful and fulfilling to him. Meanwhile, the husband chooses to treat his wife in ways that are meaningful and fulfilling to her. Neither waits for the other before acting.

> I have learned that the supernatural power of God's love can empower me to do the impossible and the uncomfortable.

I am convinced we cannot have a deep, awesome marriage without the supernatural power of Christ working in our lives. I don't think it's possible. But here's some good news: I have learned that the supernatural power of God's love can empower me to do the impossible and the uncomfortable. With God's help, I can give my wife what she needs that doesn't come easy for me. I admit that the struggle often comes because at the core I am a selfish guy. But I'm also letting God change my heart. Over the years I've learned to give what I know says "I love you" to her, even after I've been wounded or she has failed to meet my expectations. And, in like manner, I've watched her love me even when I have been most unlovable. No, it's not easy; but it's definitely worth it!

In case you think I'm overstating the case for *agape* love, I'd like to share a little story that illustrates beautifully what can happen when a person begins to implement this new paradigm of love toward their mate. The fellow, apparently a stockbroker working on Wall Street, wrote the following account of an eventful vacation.

I made a vow to myself on our drive to the beach cottage. For two weeks I would try to be a loving husband and father—no "ifs, ands, or buts." The idea had come to me as I was listening to a Bible teacher on the radio. He was quoting a passage. He said husbands ought to be thoughtful to their wives. Then he went on to say that love is an act of the will and that we choose to love.

I had to admit that I had been a pretty selfish husband and that our love had been pretty dull, mostly due to my own insensitivity, often in petty ways. Getting mad at my wife for her tardiness. Insisting that my channel was the one that we watch. Throwing away day-old papers even though I knew she hadn't read them. For two weeks I was going to change all that. And I did. When we headed out the door, I kissed my wife and said, "That new yellow sweater looks great on you."

"Oh, Tom, you noticed," she said, surprised.

After the long drive, I wanted to sit and read. She suggested we take a walk on the beach. I started to refuse and then I thought, *She's been alone with the kids all week and now she wants to be alone with me.* We walked on the beach while the children flew their kites.

So it went, two weeks without calling the Wall Street investment firm in which I'm a director. I usually hate museums, and we went to the shell museum and I enjoyed it. I even held my tongue when, as usual, she made us all late for dinner. I decided to be relaxed and happy and that's how the whole vacation passed. I made a vow to keep on remembering to choose love. Just like Jesus in the Garden of Gethsemane, I didn't always feel like it, but I did it because it was right. There was one thing that went wrong with my experiment, however. My wife and I still laugh about it today. On the last night at our cottage, preparing for bed, my wife stared at me with the saddest expression.

"What's the matter?" I asked her.

"Tom, do you know something I don't know?"

"What do you mean?"

"That checkup I had several weeks ago. That doctor, did he tell you something about me? Tom, you've been so good to me. Am I going to die?"

It took a moment for it to sink in, and then I said, "No, honey, you're not dying, I'm just starting to live."

Conclusion

Here's the deal. You can have that. Love isn't a feeling; it's a choice. As you learn to make the right choices and trust God, you'll have feelings you never thought possible. But the paradigm is different. This is God's design for marriage that is far different from the descriptions and assumptions that are made day after day by the media. So when the strong feelings sneak up on you, when you see someone intriguing, when you meet someone's eyes and your IQ begins to drain away, **how do you know whether this is a relationship that God is orchestrating and he has produced this chemistry to draw you to this person, or whether it's just plain old infatuation?** You need to be able to answer that question if you want to break out of the vicious cycle of rotating relationships. That will be the subject of our next chapter.

Personal Evaluation

1. How would you describe in one sentence the unique aspects of each of the three kinds of love we talked about in this chapter: *eros, phileo, agape?*

2. What part does each of these aspects of love play in your present relationship (if you are married) or your expectations of married life (if you are single)?

3. Why is it so important to know the difference between infatuation and love when it comes to understanding some of your responses to members of the opposite sex?

4. Why is "falling in love" called "tricky business" in this chapter?

5. What specific steps do you sense God would have you take in order to make *agape* love a more significant part of your relationships?

5

How to Know If You're in Love

TWELVE TESTS

Do you remember the first time it happened? You caught one another's eyes, and then you looked a second time. Something inside you wanted to glance a third time, followed quickly by a fourth lingering look. You didn't want to stare, but something irresistibly drew you to that other person. When you were finally introduced, your palms were sweaty and you hoped no one noticed the increased perspiration under your arms. Your heart began to race as an exhilarating but unfamiliar feeling swept over you.

You were suddenly afraid to say anything because you knew that if you opened your mouth, out would flow incomprehensible babble. The experience was exciting and terrifying at the same time.

As the other person began to speak, you felt drawn like a magnet to a steel ingot. You didn't know her or where she came from, but something about the way she looked and the aura that she projected triggered an unexplainable feeling of euphoria and excitement. Her smile or a tiny gesture became instantly engraved in your mind. You knew you would never forget her. For an instant you wondered how you would describe this moment to a friend. Then a phrase came to mind, as if by magic, provided by countless hours of exposure to the Hollywood formula—"I think I'm falling in love."

You've been there. I've been there. No doubt we all agree that those are thrilling moments, especially if we sense a similar response from the other person. But is it really love? How do you know whether what I just described is the beginning of the greatest relationship you will ever experience on earth or simply an episode of infatuation? How do you know if you're really in love or simply physically attracted to a member of the opposite sex? In this chapter I want to give you twelve tests that will help you understand if you are in love or if, in fact, you are experiencing what relational experts call *infatuation*.

If you are a single person, your eyes may be a little wider and your mind has kicked into overdrive. Imagine! Twelve legitimate tests that can help you discern if you're really in love or not. Well, these are very good tests and they really do work. But this chapter is not just for single people who are dating or those who are engaged. It also will help anyone not in a significant relationship learn what kind of person to pursue and whom to avoid.

If you're married and you are tempted to say, "I've been married for twenty-seven years so what's this got to do with me," please think again. Our failure to understand the difference between love and infatuation goes well beyond finding the right person. Unless you understand the radical difference between love and infatuation, you may set yourself up for devastation in your future years of marriage. If you believe that what we will call infatuation is the real test of love, you may be in a very good relationship but feel unloved. Your skewed expectations may be robbing you of a rich, warm, and deep relationship. Furthermore, if you are unclear about the difference between love and infatuation, you may find yourself getting unintentionally connected to a member of the opposite sex who is not your spouse, naively concluding that you've now found "true love."

This chapter is for singles, those who are single again, and married people too. So don't skip this one. I mean that seriously. Even if you're a grandparent, you need to read this one to counsel those granddaughters and grandsons about how to wisely choose a mate with whom to build a lasting relationship.

Twelve Tests of Love

Each of these tests is designed to help you **discern and distinguish between love and infatuation.** After you read each statement, apply it to your present relationship, or to your expectations of what a love relationship should include. Ask yourself this question: *Is my current relationship or my view of relationships more in alignment with love or with infatuation in this particular area?* In fact, I encourage you to take a pencil or pen and write an "L" for love and an "I" for infatuation alongside each of the tests. If your relationship is over 51 percent love by the standard of the test, write an "L" in the margin; if it's 51 percent or more on the infatuation side, put an "I." This isn't a test that you can fail. This is a tool to help you learn and grow in your understanding of the most important part of life—loving another human being. So without any further ado, let's jump in and take the tests together.

> This is a tool to help you learn and grow in your understanding of the most important part of life— loving another human being.

1. The Test of Time

Love benefits and grows through time; infatuation ebbs and diminishes with time. Infatuation may come suddenly. We find ourselves thinking, "Boom! I'm in love." That's actually infatuation. We probably ought to make an effort to avoid speaking about "falling in love." We can fall into infatuation, we can fall into lust, but we most truthfully *grow* into love. Love develops out of relationship and caring and core personal character traits, not our instant impression or perception of another person. Infatuation can explode at any moment, but real love takes time. More than one wise person has advised not to declare love until a reasonable amount of time has passed.

Are you in a rush to label certain feelings "love," or do you have other words to describe feelings? Do you save the word *love* for something better than feelings? How much time do you think needs to pass before love can be clearly identified? If you find yourself "falling in love" often and early, only to be later disappointed, perhaps remembering this first test of real love will save you future heartache.

---

2. The Test of Knowledge

Love grows out of an appraisal of all the known characteristics of the other person. Infatuation may grow out of an acquaintance with only one of these characteristics known about the other person. Something about the way that person looks or the way he or she functions in a certain role may give you a very distorted idea of their full character. You may not even know the other person. Frankly, a glance or a chance meeting can act as a kind of trigger that sets off the chemicals.

I'm amazed how often couples who are well into planning their weddings display a lack of basic knowledge about each other. When I ask each of them to give me a detailed introduction of their mate, you would often think they were introducing a stranger. I then ask them to give me several examples of personal character traits that they have come to appreciate in the other person, with illustrations. Again, I get clichés: "He's got a great sense of humor" or "She's always 'there' for me" or an embarrassed silence. I often say, "You know, I've stopped asking couples why they are getting married. I mean, there's only one answer, right?" They smile, knowingly. I continue, "The expected answer is, 'Because we're in love.'" They nod—that's what they were planning to say. "Now, if almost all couples say that, but at least half of them end up getting a divorce, then that's not a very compelling reason to get married, is it?" They look at each other, wondering where this is going. "What good reasons," I ask, "other than saying 'we're in love,' can you give me to explain why you are getting married?" Unfortunately, most couples seldom have shared goals, shared vision, or shared purposes for where they expect to go together in their marriage.

Infatuation lives in a make-believe world where the object of our affection is perfect, flawless, and completely devoted to us. Infatuation is happy to know very little. Love longs to know well. Love wants to study the other person's needs, desires, dreams, and hopes because it wants to do everything to make them a reality. Love is interested, not in what it can get, but in what it can give. The development of a relationship ought to be like an undergraduate degree in which the other person becomes a multifaceted and fascinating study. Marriage, then, becomes a lifelong pursuit of a Ph.D. in knowing and understanding your spouse.

How well do you expect to know the person you marry? Or how well do you know your spouse? Can you describe your wife's or husband's central purpose in life? Can you list three objectives he or she would like to accomplish in the next five years? What unusual event or place would he or she most like to experience sometime in his or her lifetime? Have you decided how you can best help him or her achieve that goal or dream? Infatuation quickly decides it knows everything it needs to know. Genuine love creates an atmosphere of such interest that the other person opens like a flower. How are you doing in the love test of knowledge?

---

3. The Test of Focus

Genuine love is other-person centered. Infatuation is self-centered. You know what infatuated people are all caught up with? Themselves. I watched a roommate in college discover the power of infatuation for the first time. The Greeks were right—he went a little insane. When it started, I was happy for him because he was shy and didn't have many relationships. It was surprising to hear him say, "Oh, Chip, she's just amazing. I've never been in love like this before."

About the tenth time he made a version of that statement, I asked, "So, what's her name? Do I know her?"

He smiled sheepishly, "Oh, I haven't actually met her yet. I'm still working up the courage to find out her name."

"Well, how do you know you're in love?" I asked.

He answered, "Man, when she walks across campus, you wouldn't believe the feelings I get just watching her."

> You know what
> infatuated people
> are all caught up
> with? Themselves.

I won't bore you with the details, but this went on for days. He eventually managed an introduction; then our conversations took on a new tone of urgency. He would stand, half-dressed, in our dorm room, asking somewhat confused questions: "Chip, what do you think looks better, this shirt or that one? What about these shoes? I've got my basketball shoes—I could wear them. I might see her today." Every time we talked it was about how he was going to look, how he was going to come off, what kind of impression he was going to make. I admit I had my own set of relational dysfunctions, but even I could see (infatuation is almost always more obvious in someone else's life) that he was suffering from some kind of fever or virus. What was his focus? *Himself.* That's not love; that's chemical exchanges of the brain. Infatuation.

In your most important relationships, to what degree is your attention focused on what *you* are receiving from them and to what degree is your attention focused on meeting the *other's* needs? Do you think about how you're going to look and feel in the relationship, or about what you can do to make that person look and feel great?

---

4. The Test of Singularity

Genuine love is focused on only one person. An infatuated individual may be "in love" with two or more persons

simultaneously. Unfortunately, all my best stories about the silly things people do when they are infatuated feature me as the main character.

During my first year out of college, I was dating a girl still in school at another college. Most of what we had was infatuation. I didn't know her very well, but we were building a little relationship. We weren't even seriously dating, but I was beginning to think that maybe she was "the one" because I was having these feelings.

Meanwhile, I ended up on a Christian basketball team that traveled all over South America. At our first stop in Puerto Rico we played a good team in a big stadium. After the game I met this really nice girl who was a missionary there, and we ended up going on a very romantic picnic together. I can still remember the color of her dress. I also remember that I had feelings. I found myself attracted to her. My response caught me by surprise because the feelings were similar to those I was having toward "my girl at home."

Then we flew to Peru where our missionary host had a daughter a year or two younger than I. She was cute in a "you just have to look twice" way. I fell instantly in love with her. Suddenly, I couldn't remember what "my girl at home" looked like.

When we got to Santiago, Chile, we were welcomed with a huge dinner. I don't remember the food, but I do recall the girl who sat across from me with dark brown eyes, beautiful, long, black hair, and a sparkling smile. Her laughter made up for the fact that I couldn't understand anything she said to me in Spanish. I did my own translations, and it turned out that everything she said to me was highly complimentary of my skills and appearance. She never saw it, but I handed my heart across the table to her about halfway through the meal.

We visited five countries in a few weeks and I ended up in love with five different girls plus the girl from back home. Do you know what I learned? I learned that what I *felt* had practically nothing to do with *love*. It was all about chemicals. I could be attracted to a lot of different people, but that wasn't love. My infatuation switch was simply stuck in the "ON" position.

But lest you think infatuation is simply a harmless emotional game played by the young, consider the impact of infatuation during one of those seasons of marriage when life gets hard or dull and marital love grows a little cold. Circumstances, changes, and mistakes add up to make relationships an enterprise of ongoing work. And when the going gets tough in marriage, the pain often seems to outweigh the rewards. You have your first child. Then you have another one and you've got two kids in diapers. Then you've got a boss who really pushes you at work. Or your babies suddenly hit the teenage years and life takes on a new set of pressures. You feel like you're expending every ounce of energy dealing with a rebellious child. Financial pitfalls and windfalls show up at various times along the way, each having their own set of complications. Then, when you hit the empty nest, you discover you haven't really cultivated and stoked the coals of your relationship. During any one of these predictable seasons in a marriage, the emotional parts of the relationship can feel weak and empty.

> One of the side effects of stale times in marriage is vulnerability to infatuation.

Deeply committed partners who are Christians and love each other are not immune from such times. Even those in a great marriage can be caught off guard by an unexpectedly difficult time. Knowing how good and meaningful marriage can be makes it difficult to deal with times when it isn't. One of the side effects of stale times in marriage is vulnerability to infatuation. You're not vulnerable because you're a bad person; you're vulnerable because you're vulnerable. When feelings have temporarily dried up from one direction, it's hard not to pay attention to feelings coming from another direction. The following scenario can begin at almost any moment.

A woman goes to a Bible study and on her way home she glances over and sees a guy in another car. They happen to pull into the same coffee shop. He gallantly opens the door for her and says, "I guess great minds work in the same way. Had to have my coffee." Their eyes meet. She smiles in response to the courtesy and the compliment. No big deal, but his kindness and her response indicates there is chemistry. The next week she finds out that his office is in the same complex as hers because they spot each other on the way to their cars. He laughs and says something like, "Don't I know you from somewhere? Race you to the coffee shop?" Their eyes meet again. The comment sounds innocent, but to someone in a certain frame of mind, going through an empty emotional time, it holds a promise of something nice. Now that woman is a wise Christian believer who knows Christ in a deep way. She inwardly reasons she would never do anything to jeopardize her marriage or dishonor the Lord. But you can also see the attraction of infatuation. She is vulnerable, lonely, feeling unappreciated at home. She's flattered by the attention. Faced with the prospect of going home to a familiar coldness, the temptation of the unfamiliar warmth of the coffee shop and a kind stranger seem interesting. Convinced this could never lead to anything more than a casual friendship, the dance begins. What is happening is quite natural, which makes going through it unawares particularly dangerous.

A similar danger awaits the man who is under a lot of pressure at work. He may be going through a time of confusing changes. Job security, mounting expenses, growing and demanding kids that seem to consume his wife's energy, and a marriage which has developed a dullness all contribute to his vulnerability. He can't remember the last time he made love with his wife. He's frustrated but doesn't know how to talk about it. He has buried the hurt and desperation down inside. He keeps pouring himself into his work, tries to be a good dad, and finds temporary relief in an occasional round of golf and Monday night football. Then he notices someone at work who really seems to listen to him. She finds ways to be helpful and encouraging. She compliments his efforts, his skills, and how nice he looks in that shirt. He begins to look forward to spending his days at the office with her. He wonders if it would be appropriate, simply as a way of saying thank you, to suggest they have lunch together sometime. There would be no harm in it. He's been a Christian for seventeen years, serves in the church,

and has three kids. He'd never let this friendship move beyond
. . . and the dance begins.

The great majority of affairs rarely occur solely on the basis of
physical attraction. They usually start out with a little chemistry
during a time of vulnerability. But families break up because very
good, godly people simply haven't learned what to do in a situation where it suddenly feels so good to get some of that *eros* out.
They confuse infatuation with love and make foolish decisions.
Those apparently innocent and fun choices end up destroying
children, breaking up a good thing that just needed some attention, and embarking on what turns out to be a painful series of
shameful disappointments. How often does this happen? Just
look at the number of broken families that you know personally.

> If you don't know the difference between infatuation and love, you'll destroy others' lives and your own.

The life cycle of infatuation is nine to
eighteen months. Then all those breathless and wonderful feelings leave, and
you're stuck with another person with
the same kinds of needs that you have.
That person knows you can't be trusted
because you left your last mate. You know
you can't really trust them because, down
deep, you're afraid of experiencing the
kind of betrayal that you inflicted on someone else. What's left are
two unhappy people struggling with character flaws. If you don't
know the difference between infatuation and love, you'll destroy
others' lives and your own.

How did you grade yourself on the test of singularity? In what
ways have you realized that it's much easier to work on problems
in an existing relationship where singularity and faithfulness are
maintained than to create a whole new set of problems with another person?

5. The Test of Security

**Genuine love requires and fosters a sense of security and
feelings of trust.** An infatuated individual seems to have a blind

sense of security, based upon wishful thinking rather than careful consideration; infatuation is blind to problems. Or he or she may have a sense of insecurity that is sometimes expressed as jealousy. Security grows and flows out of deep awareness of the other person's character, values, and track record. You know who he or she really is. And when you know who they really are, you trust them. You are not jealous because you know their heart is yours. Jealousy is often a sign of a lack of trust, and a lack of trust is a sign of infatuation in real life.

What role does jealousy play in your relationship? How would you describe the level of security that you experience in your relationship? How do problems affect the level of security you experience in your relationship? Genuine love considers everything involved in the relationship with the other person, not just immediate feelings or momentary problems.

6. The Test of Work

An individual in love works for the other person, for his or her mutual benefit. By contrast, an infatuated person loses his or her ambition, appetite, and interests in everyday affairs. A woman in love may study to make her husband proud. A man in love may have his ambitions spurred on by planning and saving for the future together. Partners in genuine love may daydream about the potential of their relationship, but their daydreams are reasonably attained. People in infatuation only think of their own misery. They often daydream of unrealistic objectives and ideals that neither they nor their partner could ever actually attain. Sometimes the dreams become substitutes for reality and each individual lives in a world of his or her own imagination.

Have you ever been around someone who's terminally infatuated? They used to go to work on time and they used to be very faithful. They used to be the kind of person who had a regular schedule and exhibited dependable behavior. If they made a commitment, they meant it. But then they caught "the love bug" and everything changed. They suddenly live in chaos. That's not love; that's brain damage. Infatuation.

When you love someone, you have an accurate appraisal of the relationship and you work at it. If you're in a relationship and the other person is glassy-eyed all the time so that he or she can't get anything done, suspect infatuation. If you know you need to save some money and you're working at the problem, but they won't, there's a danger that you may not be involved in genuine love. Infatuation lives off the relationship; love builds into the relationship.

When it comes to working on your relationship and working for your partner, what grade ("L" or "I") does your relationship get?

---

7. The Test of Problem Solving

A couple in love faces problems frankly and tries to solve them. Infatuated people tend to disregard or try to ignore problems. If there are barriers to getting married for a couple in love, those barriers are approached and removed. The barriers that cannot be removed may be circumvented with knowledge. They do not go into marriage blindly. They handle problems with clear, shared decisions. On the other hand, friends and family may be astonished at the foolishness and blindness of infatuated people.

About four or five times a year I get approached by a type of couple I can spot now almost before they speak to me. They walk up wearing what I call "the goofy glow." They're usually holding hands and tripping over chairs because they can't stop looking longingly into each other's eyes. "We're in love," they begin. It goes downhill quickly from there. "We met yesterday (or last week, or two weeks ago). God showed us we're meant to be together. Could you do the marriage?"

"When?" I ask, trying to work toward some sense of reality in the conversation.

"Tomorrow, this week—as soon as possible," they respond.

"Why then? How exactly did this come about?" I ask.

"Well," she sighs, "I dropped my purse and he picked it up and our eyes met. Then I found out that his last name started with an S, and I prayed for someone whose last name starts with S, so there—we know it's from God."

Before I can express my amazement, she babbles on, "What's so incredible is that even though he's thirty-eight years older than me and I'm not sure if he's a Christian, God has made it so clear that he's the one. We don't have a common vision, but we'll figure that out later. I don't know anything about his family other than he's been married seventeen times. Ours would be a blended family because I have eleven children and he has seven, but we love each other. It'll work out."

I'm obviously exaggerating, but it comes out almost like that. What is it? It's infatuation mixed with classic denial—with an added pinch of insanity. Such a relationship isn't based on communication, genuine knowledge, geography, core values, commitment, or spiritual vision. In fact, these essential components are almost completely lacking or ignored. You say that you love each other so it will work, but wait until you wake up and you realize that all you had was infatuation. Genuine love, contrary to popular belief, isn't blind. It sees very clearly. Infatuation, on the other side, exists almost completely in the dark.

How good are you and your partner at seeing problems and working on them? Do you find that you gloss over hard issues in your relationship or face them squarely? What obstacles and barriers do you and your partner feel good about facing and overcoming in your relationship?

---

8. The Test of Distance

Love knows the importance of distance. Infatuation imagines love to be intense closeness, 24/7, all the time. I often counsel those who are dating to go on a short-term mission trip or take on a project that will require them to work alone. If circumstances require you to be temporarily separated from the one you love, that will teach you a lot about the quality of your relationship. In terms of distance, if you're in a long-term relation-ship right now and you call each other three, four, or five times a day, or you just have to see each other every day, that's not a good sign. That means you're trying to keep the chemicals alive. If there is not a sense of separateness, a distinct life, relationships with other people, and healthy balance, then the relationship is probably a lot more infatuation than it is love.

One of the best things that happened during my courtship time with Theresa was a trip I took to the Philippines for six weeks. I participated in another basketball tour. Every day we played a game in the morning and a game at night. We drove from game to game surrounded by rice paddies nearby and volcanic mountains in the distance. The places where we stopped were often little more than a couple of cement buildings in the center of a thatched hut village. I'd spend an hour each afternoon with God and really ask him to lead me and teach me in his Word. I asked God to help me restrain those things in me that needed to be restrained and to help me release those things in me that needed to be released.

> Because genuine love is not based just on emotions, some distance will often let you know what is really in your heart.

I told God I wanted to become the right person for Theresa. I grew more in love during those six weeks apart from my future wife than I ever did drinking coffee with her or being together most of the time. Because genuine love is not based just on emotions, some distance will often let you know what is really in your heart.

How does your love handle distance? Do you tend to get anxious and frustrated when you can't be together all the time? What has distance taught you about your love?

9. The Test of Physical Attraction

Physical attraction is a relatively small part of genuine love, but it is the central focus of infatuation. Now don't read "small part" to mean "not a part" in what I just stated. If your heart doesn't skip a beat now and then and you don't feel real attraction for your mate or the person you plan to marry, I'd call that a problem. Let's not make genuine love so spiritual that we deny reality and God's Word. Sexual attraction definitely has a part in love.

As I've already said, our culture holds up a magnifier to physical attraction and makes it the primary purpose of love. Our culture tells us to take the shortest and quickest route to sexual fulfillment as the best way to find love. But that route is a destructive detour. By leaving out the other two foundational components of giving love and friendship love, we miss much of the fullness and sustainable aspects of physical attraction. Genuine love requires all three kinds of love, but physical attraction takes a relatively smaller role when a couple is building a healthy relationship. Infatuation, however, makes physical attraction the very test of love itself.

In contrast, I've noticed an important characteristic about couples in genuine love. For them, any physical contact they have tends to have special meaning as well as pleasure. Couples often communicate volumes through looks. These tend to express what they feel toward each other. In infatuation, direct, continual physical contact tends to be an end in and of itself. Time together requires only pleasurable experiences. Infatuation tends to produce a relationship that attempts to exist on the emotional equivalent of a continual sugar rush.

We've been effectively brainwashed to believe that attraction is the surest test of whether or not we are in love. Actually, when we are attracted to someone, it doesn't mean that we are in love at all. It simply means that the person to whom we're attracted is good looking. There is a chemical response and something inside us goes, "Wow!" I've already demonstrated that if we find four or five other really good-looking people in the same day at different times, we'll hear that same internal voice say "Wow!" to them, too. That's not love. We're just exercising our unpredictable capacity for infatuation. Instead of recognizing such feelings for what they are, people choose to get physically involved with people who are virtual strangers. The moment you get physically and emotionally involved, you will find your ability to think clearly and objectively evaporates. This makes for very unstable relationships.

In contrast to this pattern, people in genuine love aren't trying to get their own lustful fulfillment. Their words and actions tell the other, "I have your best interests in mind." The physical components enter a relationship when they can communicate clearly. That means, for example, that a woman starts to hold hands in a relationship to communicate that there is trust developing. It's bringing the relationship to a deeper level than just being friends. When you kiss someone, there is meaning beyond the physical act. The questions shouldn't be "When should kissing begin: on the first or second, ninth or tenth date?" or "How far can I go?" or "How soon can I get my selfish needs met and have a pleasurable experience that feels really good?" That's a very limited view and it's not love. The real question is "As we take every step in the physical bonding chain, what are we discovering and communicating about ourselves and our mutual commitment to God and to each other?"

What we have in our day is just the opposite. People are bonding physically before they even know each other and then trying to work through all the struggles that get bypassed along the way. The results are disastrous. People get wounded. Relationships disintegrate. People learn not to trust—the very foundation needed for love to grow.

Eventually we're going to talk in this book about the difference between sex and love. We tend to think sex and love equal the same thing. Wrong! Sex is great. Love is great. They're not the same thing. Each has its place in a relationship.

How many positive aspects and joys in your relationship can you list that have nothing to do with physical attraction or closeness? Apart from physical attraction, how would your mate say he or she knows that you love him or her?

---

10. The Test of Affection

In love affection is expressed later in the relationship, involving the external expression of the physical attraction we just

described. In infatuation affection is expressed earlier, sometimes at the very beginning. Affection tends to push toward greater and greater physical intimacy. Without the control of the other aspects of genuine love, affection spends itself quickly. It gives the appearance of making the relationship "close," but the closeness is artificial and fragile. When affection flows out of deep understanding and growing friendship, it gains in meaning and value.

Since in all likelihood your mate experiences being loved in a different way than you do, to what extent do you and your mate use affection as a way of showing each other that you understand the other's needs? In your relationship, how is affection balanced out by friendship love and giving love?

---

11. The Test of Stability

Love tends to endure. Infatuation may change suddenly and unpredictably. In infatuation the wind blows here and you're in love. The wind blows there and you're in love. Not so with real love. Real love is stable. There is commitment. I will say more on this topic later. For now, the test of stability can hardly be applied to a relationship measured in days or weeks. So how do you test stability? Society suggests we test it by living together. For reasons we will look at later, living together actually promotes instability rather than stability.

The best way to test stability in a new relationship comes through knowing that person in the context of his or her other relationships. How is he or she in relation to parents, friends, and siblings? Frankly, someone who has been married more than once ought to expect to be calmly and seriously tested when it comes to the question of stability.

Perhaps one of the first and best questions to ask as you think about testing stability in your relationship is this: How would I demonstrate to my partner that I have developed the characteristic of stability in my relationships? What's your track record in relationships? What is your partner's? Is there a pattern that raises confidence or warning signals?

12. The Test of Delayed Gratification

A couple in genuine love is not indifferent to the timing of their wedding, but they do not feel an irresistible drive toward it. An infatuated couple tends to feel an urge to get married—instantly. Postponement for the infatuated is intolerable. Why is this? Why wouldn't a couple wait and do it at the right time in the right way? Why wouldn't a couple want to deal with the real issues so they could have a solid marriage? These questions reveal the difference between love and infatuation.

Two Bible couples offer us a sharp contrast of these two approaches: Amnon and Tamar (whose story is told in 2 Samuel 13) and Jacob and Rachel (whose story you will find in Genesis 29:1–20).

Amnon represents a guy who couldn't wait. He had a case of consuming infatuation; he was obsessed with Tamar. When he took by force what he thought he wanted, his "love" vanished like smoke. He couldn't wait, and it spelled destruction in his own life as well as Tamar's.

Jacob was attracted to Rachel almost immediately. Yet he had to work seven years in order to marry Rachel. That's five years beyond the typical lifespan of infatuation. Do you think his love understood stability and delayed gratification? The Bible says that the seven years "seemed like only a few days." Why? "Because of his love for her." It wasn't about his lustful needs; it was about something really worth waiting for.

As you enter into a potentially serious relationship, ask yourself if your pace is based in fear or faith. Is your pace based on anxiety over deprivation and physical drives, or is your pace the result of a desire for careful and thorough preparation for marriage?

Using the Twelve Tests

How did you do in these tests? Did you find yourself wanting to put "L" for love next to most of the test points but admitting, like most of us, that you had to put "I" for infatuation beside several of them? Isn't it amazing how much Hollywood has influenced your thinking and mine? I hope these tests were not a "downer" but a process that has helped you see more clearly the differences between love and infatuation. They will continue to offer you help in your present relationships, your future ones, and your marriage.

I'll let you in on a secret. Now that we are in our third decade of marriage, one of the amazing things about my relationship with my wife is that I keep falling in love with her. In fact, the longer and the better I learn to love her, the more I discover that the brain chemicals work in ways I never could have predicted even ten years ago. It's not that we're pitting love against infatuation—it's simply that we want to understand the difference so we can enjoy each one in its special place in a relationship. You see, love in a lasting relationship is not a long, gradual decline from the peak of our heady initial romance. Lasting love is more like standing where the ocean meets the shore—the waves keep coming in. Not every wave of emotion is the same, and that turns out to be very interesting and exciting. But it takes time and commitment to discover the wonder of a lasting relationship. Yes, the waves and the tides ebb and flow. But when we know what love really is, we also know that the waves and the tide will return. So stay at the beach! Learn to "read the waves." Work through the relational issues and enjoy the varied sounds and passion of the crashing or softly lapping surf. Too many people walk away from relationships without ever getting their feet wet!

Using a similar picture, let me say that many people make the mistake of thinking that real love is like a swimming pool—something they fall or jump into. Rather than having the dynamic and varied experience of the oceanfront love, they leap right into the deep end of the pool, thinking that strong feelings, light-headedness, and physical attraction must be a sure sign of love. They discover sooner or later that a great *desire* to swim doesn't mean much if we've never learned *how* to swim. Watching movies of great swimmers doesn't make us like them. But if wanting to swim gets us serious about swimming lessons, then the thrill of buoyancy and the joy of weightless freedom that swimming (and genuine love) can bring will be ours. Think of the details and insights you've been learning in this book as "swimming lessons" so that you can enjoy love.

Here is my heartfelt, pastoral encouragement to each single person reading these words: Decide you are going to base your life on more than appearances and advertisements. As tempting as it may be to jump into relationships without forethought, stop long enough to ask whether you really want the results that the Hollywood formula delivers or whether you want to be one of those who pursue the adventure of doing love God's way.

As I've noted repeatedly, this will not be an easy choice. You will be bucking a powerful and often unseen trend. But I assure you that those who are following God's prescription can report measurably better results than the world offers.

So where do we go from here? The next two chapters address one of the most important issues in living and loving God's way. We've gotten confused about the differences between love and sex. We've forgotten how and when they fit together. As we will see, recognizing the differences between love and sex really does make all the difference!

Personal Evaluation

1. As you review the twelve tests for recognizing love, which three do you find it easiest to practice in a relationship?

2. Which three tests indicate that some aspects of your relationship are rooted in infatuation rather than genuine love?

3. How does having these twelve measurable factors help you in evaluating your present (or future) relationships?

4. What one test provided the greatest personal challenge to the way you think about "being in love"? What specific action steps might help you to meet that challenge?

6

Love and Sex

KNOWING THE DIFFERENCE MAKES
ALL THE DIFFERENCE

N ow that we have looked at the differences between love and infatuation, we are ready to look at the riskiest part of the risky business of falling in love. Those who don't take time to understand the difference between love and sex discover painfully that the differences matter. We live in a sex-saturated culture. But the messages and impressions about sex we pick up from our surroundings somehow change when we try to live that way. Sex isn't at all simple. Love is complicated. Relationships get messy. When we fail to understand the difference between love and sex, we are destined to ruin both.

Lauren and Mike's Story

Drs. Les and Leslie Parrott, in their book *Relationships,* describe a sadly typical experience lived out by a young couple they call

Lauren and Mike. These two college students, adrift in the somewhat unreal world of school, spent hours alone staring at each
other, studying, talking—oblivious to the rest of the world. Several months into their relationship, a memorable event occurred.
They arrived late one evening at Mike's apartment and Lauren
discovered they had the place to themselves. Mike announced
this intimate privacy as if he knew already that Lauren had been
waiting for this moment.

Almost immediately, Mike began to kiss Lauren passionately,
whispering about her beauty and his intense desire to know all
of her. He repeatedly declared his love and said he wanted them
to show each other how much love they shared. He clearly had
more on his mind than she was prepared for that evening. After
hearing her tell her story, the Parrotts described her inner turmoil
in those moments:

> Lauren's mind started to whirl . . . as he led her to his bedroom.
> "Mike believed in me, when no one else would," she later told us.
> "I wasn't planning to have sex that night but I knew that the future
> of our relationship would probably be over if we weren't intimate
> soon." During the next several months Lauren became consumed
> with Mike. "He was all that mattered," as she put it. Sex soon
> became part of all their dates. But when Lauren began talking about
> changing her summer plans to be with Mike, his passion quickly
> cooled. . . . It was no real surprise that Lauren and Mike broke up
> before the end of the spring semester.[1]

Lauren's story echoes millions of others. Statistics indicate that
as many as 83 percent of young women admit they did not plan
or anticipate their first sexual encounter.[2] Apparently, the majority
of these women felt pressured by circumstances or so caught up
in the flow of passion that they couldn't stop themselves. Notice
Lauren's confusion at the moment of decision. She went along
with Mike because she concluded in that moment that "the future
of our relationship would probably be over if we weren't intimate
soon." Follow carefully Lauren's logic: "I love Mike. I must give
him sex or I will lose this relationship." She had no clear distinc-

tion between love and sex. Her premise was, sex will keep our love alive! Sex became a bargaining chip in the relationship, perhaps the most important one. Her confusion led to a bad choice. She did something she wasn't ready to do because she thought she was less ready to risk ending the relationship by saying no.

I chose Lauren and Mike's story because, like every relationship story, it has two sides. The Parrotts also interviewed Mike. They discovered some interesting differences when they compared his perspective on their relationship with Lauren's.

For Mike, the first four months of their relationship had produced a very close relationship in which they could talk about anything and everything. Each of them shared very painful parts of their past with the other. In Mike's mind, the sharing meant they cared deeply for each other. Along with the intimate conversations, they also shared long episodes of physical intimacy that, though intense and enjoyable, always stopped short of intercourse. Mike admitted that the possibility and desire for sex had been on his mind, though they had never directly discussed having intercourse. He guessed that it would be just another phase of their relationship that would be a natural byproduct of their growing love. He confessed to moving the relationship in that direction by flirtatious comments, like suggesting it might be fun to bathe together sometime, to which, he said, Lauren simply laughed. Whatever she meant by her response, Mike didn't read it as negative. In fact, as the Parrotts report:

> All this nebulous and flirtatious talk gave Mike the idea that as they were falling in love, sex would be a natural expression of their love. "In my line of thinking," Mike said, "sex is a way of expressing feelings you can't express with words. Believe me, I'm not the kind of guy who's looking for a one-night stand; I'm not going to jump in the sack with just anybody." He told us how "honoring" women was important to him and that he would never "use" a woman to get sex. . . . "It's weird," Mike told us. "Once Lauren wanted to change her summer plans just to be with me I began to feel smothered."[3]

Like Lauren, Mike had an explanation for his actions: If you really love someone, sex will be the natural expression of that love. He saw no implied or lasting commitment in intercourse. It was simply crossing the next bridge in a journey whose destination he wasn't ready to consider. He was unprepared for the new world he discovered when he crossed the bridge of intercourse. Crossing that bridge forced him to consider a commitment he wasn't ready to make.

Research indicates that once an uncommitted couple gets involved in sexual intercourse, the relationship usually begins to end. They have reached the superficial end of the physical aspects of the relationship, and they have no particularly compelling reason to explore its depths. Unlike Lauren's premise, Mike's message was: Love sanctifies sex. In other words, if you think you love each other, sex is okay, even if you're not married. He lost the girl that he loved because sex completely changed the dynamic of their relationship. The kind of commitment that the act of sex meant for her, he wasn't ready for. She crossed the bridge of sexual intercourse with the intention of living on the other side. He wanted to keep crossing the bridge without making the commitment to settle down. Lauren thought that you had to give sex to get love, and giving sex would make the relationship continue. She was wrong. Mike thought the natural way to express love would be sex, whether you were committed to one another or not. He was wrong.

I've counseled many Laurens and Mikes over the years, and I've cried with them in their pain. Their story is so common, yet it astounds me how often it is repeated by Christians and non-Christians alike in relationship after relationship. I've looked into the eyes of countless couples, young and old, who have traveled the road of falling in love, sharing deeply, having sex, and then breaking up. They wrongly assume the problem was the other person rather than a fundamental misunderstanding by both of them about how sex impacts a relationship. Even when everything seems to be going fine in the sexual arena, there can be, as we will see next, some long-term effects to sexual choices that deserve our attention.

Another Kind of Sex Story

Counselor Paula Reinhart sits quietly and listens. In two separate counseling sessions, she hears about the long-term effects on people's lives after years of living with the Hollywood formula for love, sex, and lasting relationships. As you read these real-life accounts, ponder carefully how our inability to distinguish between love and sex can impact our future.

In her first session of the day, Paula listens to the account of a woman who is barely twenty years old but seems to carry a lifetime of heaviness on her shoulders. She comes to Paula resentful because she thinks she ought to be able to handle things on her own. She confesses her life is a mess. Her current boyfriend is insensitive and her divorced father has married a woman she can't stand. While she's describing these relationships, she muses about God's place in her life. Trying to make some headway in talking about her present situation, Paula asks several questions about her relationship with her boyfriend, including whether or not she sleeps with her boyfriend. She answers yes, annoyed that Paula had to ask, and then reflects about her sexual history. She eventually mentions her loss of virginity.

> "I didn't want to have a bad experience in losing my virginity—like some of my friends," she says. "So I found a guy I knew but didn't feel anything special for, and I had sex with him. That way I could just get it over with."
>
> *Your virginity was something you wanted to "just get over"?*
>
> "Well, sure. That way I would enjoy sex more with guys I really cared about." These words explain her logic, one alien to my own but so representative of the sexual world of her generation. Losing one's virginity, in many cases, is a girl's rite of passage into relationships and sex—where, it seems, all the happy people live.[4]

Paula then describes a second appointment that same day with a woman named Molly, who is a decade older than the first woman. The lifestyle that seemed so casual, sensual, and unending at twenty has taken on a different tone at thirty.

Molly's personal portfolio includes a husband, children, a job, and an underlying difficulty she hopes Paula can help her resolve. Molly has no desire for sex. She loves her husband but can hardly bring herself to participate in intercourse with him. Her lack of interest causes friction, and it spills into other areas of life. She reports that many arguments with her mate are really thinly veiled expressions of frustration with their sex life. She wants help. Paula decides she needs to find out more about Molly's past.

So I begin to probe her sexual history and discover that she's had sex since she was 16, with as many as 10 men, one of whom is now her husband. But that is the past. . . . She's reformed her life. She doesn't see why her past, even one with multiple partners, should have much bearing on her present sexual experience. I ask her a question: "Can you picture what it would have felt like to be really cherished by a man, to be so special to him that he wanted to protect your innocence? . . ."

A little trail of tears slides down her cheek, the best clue to the sense of loss she feels as she connects her early promiscuity with the boredom she now experiences.[5]

> If we fail to understand the difference between love and sex, we are doomed to failure in both our relationships and our sexuality.

In each one of the stories above, the people were confused about the difference between love and sex. When the first woman was a teenager, virginity was an almost shameful inconvenience to be quickly removed so that sex could become a regular aspect of her relationships, about as significant as a handshake. She wonders why, at age twenty, life has become mechanical, impersonal, and meaningless. Meanwhile, the thirty-year-old who could be her older sister says, "I'm a Christian now and my sexuality is part of my past life I want to forget. I indulged in sex just like gorging myself on candy. Now I can hardly stand the taste. The fact that sex is very important to my husband creates confusion for me."

These two women have a lot in common with Lauren and Mike. They also have a lot in common with many adults in our culture. They don't know the difference between love and sex. Their experiences give us at least one sharp warning: If we fail to understand the difference between love and sex, we are doomed to failure in both our relationships and our sexuality.

Exploring the Differences

Let's explore together the differences between love and sex. As we've already discovered, our source of information needs to be someone wiser than another confused human being. The One who created love, sex, and you and me has to be the best guide for understanding what we find confusing. How does God answer when we ask him, "What is your perspective on the difference between love and sex?"

I think God smiles patiently and answers, "Have you looked at what I wrote in my book? Have you paid attention to my prescription?"

I realize that many reading this book may not have much biblical background, so I want to share a personal word before we go on. I was not raised to think highly of the Bible. I certainly didn't turn to it for answers. I didn't go to church. In fact, I didn't open a Bible until I was eighteen. Until then, the word "Christian" simply meant people who didn't have fun and who were hypocrites. That was my personal experience. So I understand if people feel a certain amount of reservation about consulting the Bible for sex advice. People have heard so many distorted ideas that have supposedly come from the Bible that their defenses go up as soon as God's Word is mentioned. Others can't bring themselves to accept the idea that a book written at least twenty centuries ago could have anything relevant to say today.

Those are fair concerns. Can an ancient book still make sense today? Did it have something to say in the first century that you and I can apply in our world? Let me give you some historical background that may be a little surprising. In spite of what you have probably heard, we do not live in the most sex-saturated culture in history. In fact, the culture we live in has been highly influenced by the Judeo-Christian ethic. You and I have been deeply affected by some powerful moral values that shaped the development of our culture. The problems we are experiencing in many areas of life are actually the result of something good that is slowly unraveling. As a culture, we are gradually forgetting some important truths we once accepted as unconsciously as we now accept the Hollywood formula for love. As recently as fifty years ago, we had a far different understanding of marital commitment. The Hollywood formula hadn't been invented yet.

Certain past historical periods and cultures have set the bar for immorality very low. The world that first received the gospel of Christ was a horrendous mess when it came to understanding love, sex, and lasting relationships. Compared to the ancients, we have good reason to hope. And more than anything, I want to offer hope.

We've already looked at some significant verses in Ephesians, chapter 5. The apostle Paul was writing to Christians in a city that would easily out-sin any city we could mention today. Sex was so casual that it wasn't even viewed as sin in any way, shape, or form. Ephesus, like many ancient cities, hosted a religion centered on sex. Although men were expected to have a wife and children as part of a respectable portfolio, their daily lives were far from respectable. In downtown Ephesus, as in Athens or Corinth, there stood large temples, often dedicated to the worship of fertility goddesses. In Ephesus, the deity was known as Artemis, or Diana. Her temple was considered one of the seven wonders of the ancient world. Inside her temple there flourished a huge religious brothel. Worship consisted of sexual acts with the hundreds of "priestesses" who were treated like so many pieces of meat in a market. Men had sex available in the morning, afternoon, and night. If you were a male citizen of Ephesus, you had a public concubine on the side, a secret mistress for excitement, and you joined everyone else for sex at the temple whenever you wanted. Women were used, abused, and thrown away.

Given this glimpse of history, it is remarkable that people from that culture were the first recipients of Paul's instructions about the difference between love and sex and real relationships. The message was as revolutionary as it would have been if Paul were fomenting the overthrow of the Roman Empire. He was whispering against a howling wind of cultural habit—much like you and I will be if we dare to live in ways that contradict our current culture. We will hear people give us the same arguments the ancient Christians heard when they practiced God's way of love. Take, for example the comment of Cicero, in one of his more famous speeches: "If anyone thinks that young men should be forbidden this kind of love, he's very severe." I guess there must have been a catchy Latin phrase for "boys will be boys." People considered personal restraint of any kind impossible and undesirable in Paul's day. The idea that a woman was to be cherished and loved wasn't even considered. She was property. So what was Paul advocating? He was promoting a new paradigm of virtue—the value of chastity, the virtue of a man caring for a woman so much that he would be willing to protect, cherish, and love her, not just use her.

What Did Paul Say about Sex?

In Ephesians 5:3–4 the apostle Paul gives us a picture of the negative results that occur when we fail to "walk in love" or to understand the difference between love and sex.

> But do not let immorality or any impurity or greed even be named among you, as is proper among saints; and no filthiness and silly talk, or coarse jesting, which are not fitting, but rather giving of thanks. [NASB]

The command at the beginning of the verses above covers all our relationships. We are to refuse to take, exploit, cheapen, defraud, or substitute sexual activity for genuine love and authentic intimacy. In order to understand this paradigm, we've got to remember that sex is not wrong and God is no prude. Sex is not a sin to be avoided but a gift to be cherished.

You and I want genuine intimacy. We want to have relationships that matter. We long for someone to feel deeply loved because of us. We also want to be loved and cherished and cared for by someone else. We've already seen that the way to this goal involves "walking in love." Now it's time to see what not walking in love looks like. In the verses above, Paul says certain things will squelch and destroy love and break relationships. These are crucial warnings. If we are going to love somebody, we will not take, exploit, or cheapen him or her. We will not engage in sexual activity to create pseudointimacy that's false because we don't really care and we're not really committed. We won't substitute sex for authentic intimacy.

Certain words in theses verses deserve further attention: **immorality, impurity,** and **greed.** The first word comes from the Greek word *pornea,* from which we get the word *pornography*. *Pornea* refers to any sexual indulgence outside the permanent relationship of marriage. It's trying to fulfill your sexual appetite in such a way that the entire focus is on your pleasure rather than concern for the other person. The word *immorality* describes a broad range of behavior outside the bounds of God's command to "walk in love." On one hand, this term is used to declare that homosexual activity is outside the bounds of walking in love. On the other hand, the word is used to tell those who are unmarried that sex before marriage is beyond the bounds. It means that if you're married and have sex with someone other than your partner, it's outside the bounds. *Pornea* covers all sexual activity that isn't one woman, one man, inside the bounds of marriage, and warns us: Don't go there. Why? Not because it doesn't seem fun or exciting but because it's unloving and in direct violation of God's good prescription for healthy relationships. It won't deliver what it advertises.

The next word, *impurity,* means any indulgence of sex at the cost of someone else. It describes sexual behavior that defrauds, uses, or manipulates another person. Impurity refers to sexual attitudes that withhold dignity and respect for other people.

Impurity speaks to soul pollution. A person involved in impurity finds ways of using every part of life that can be a vehicle for good and an expression of love so that it becomes, instead, something dirty and shameful. Impurity in people causes them to leave an immoral smudge on everything and everyone they contact.

The third word, *greed*, in this context isn't so much about greed for money but rather sexual greed. This term describes lust that gradually consumes the person. At its worst, this attitude sees anyone else as an object to exploit for personal pleasure without regard to the damage done. Greed removes any sense of restraint from immorality and impurity.

These words apply not just to our behavior and actions but to our thought life as well. Immorality, impurity, and greed often develop in private. The habit of logging onto the Internet or vicariously participating in illicit sex through romance novels and various forms of pornography tends to slip out in our language. Our jokes, innuendos, and suggestive language reveal a darkened inner life. The longer we think a certain way, the more we will speak and act that way.

Remember what Jesus said? "Anyone who looks at a woman lustfully has already committed adultery with her in his heart" (Matt. 5:28). Jesus also described our inner life like a treasure box filled with good or evil. Our relationships consist of what we offer other people from our inner treasure (see Luke 6:45). Jesus tells us that our hearts, our minds, our focus, need to be pure. Why? Because anytime we go outside the protection of God's prescription, whether it be in our minds or in our words or in our deeds, we act in unloving ways. These are acts of consuming, taking, exploiting, and cheapening a relationship. No woman wants to be with her husband when his mind is on pictures that he's mentally downloaded from the Internet. No man wants to be with his wife if her mind is consumed by fantasies inflamed by romance novels or soap operas. Immorality, impurity, and sexual greed undermine and destroy loving, caring, intimate relationships. These vivid and strong prohibitions are not merely rules to keep but boundaries for our sexuality that protect us from separating sex from intimate, loving relationship.

In the next verse Paul gives three more things to use as a gauge of our fitness for walking in love. He tells us to reject *filthiness, silly talk,* and *coarse jesting,* which are not fitting for a believer. *Filthiness* refers to obscenities, and the background of the word has to do with shame. People who don't understand shame don't think about the impact of their words before they speak. Disrespectful and crude language without regard for those listening fits the category of filthiness. The mental pollution that we spoke about above eventually spews out in the way that person speaks. *Silly talk* describes the words of a person filled with foolish thoughts, insensitivity, and empty statements. Silly talk is not a reference to humorous and innocent faux pas but describes speaking with a lack of forethought that results in godless and impious statements. *Coarse jesting* literally means "to turn easily" and has the idea of quick and clever innuendoes or using sexual overtones to make a joke. Late night talk-show hosts and many popular comedians are masters of "coarse jesting." They seem to specialize in off-color humor and turning any comment or conversation into a sexually oriented one-liner.

To people just like you and me, God's Word says, "Don't allow sinful kinds of behavior or thoughts to enter your mind, your heart, or your relationships." Why? Because these words and actions are, at their core, the very opposite of walking in love. They are neither innocent nor harmless fun—they are destructive.

Why Giving Thanks Is So Important

The verses above tell us that each of these speaking modes (filthiness, silly talk, and coarse jesting) is to be replaced by *giving of thanks.* So how does gratefulness provide an adequate substitute for the way we typically speak and act? What's so great about giving thanks? First, thankfulness has an objective—we're thankful to someone. Second, we're thankful for something. If we develop a deep gratefulness to God for all he's done for us and given to us, we also will develop a deep respect for the way we treat what we have. Knowing that we have been made in the image of God, who loves us, how could we not be overwhelmed by the privilege of getting to know and cherish another person equally made in God's image?

When I am grateful for the relationship I have, I find it very hard to get interested in someone else. I cannot consciously be thanking God for Theresa as his special gift to me and simultaneously feed on thoughts or images of other women. And the same is true for you, whether single or married. The act of perpetually giving thanks for what God *has given you* and what he *has in store for you* is the greatest antidote against the onslaught of mental pollution that bombards all of us daily concerning this beautiful gift of sex.

So, What Is the Difference between Love and Sex?

Sex is one of the servants of love. They are different in that love is much greater than sex, but love and sex were designed to function in harmony. When love becomes a servant of sex, chaos results. Our culture has gotten confused about the difference between love and sex in two ways: (1) We have tried to separate love and sex, describing sex as a harmless and meaningless form of casual entertainment between people who have no lasting commitment, and (2) We have tried to make sex and love almost synonymous, so that great love means great sex and great sex means great love. Both mistakes have led to lives like Lauren's, Mike's, Molly's, and perhaps yours.

Facing the confusion begins the correction. Realizing we've been wrong about love and sex can be painful and shameful, but as we admit it, the change leads to hope and healing. The results are worth the difficulties. I know that what I am saying is about as countercultural as anything you could ever read. I am also aware that, even among a great majority of those who identify themselves as followers of Christ, sexual purity has become simply "one of the commands that most people don't obey." So I appeal to you: as you read the following E-mail I received from a radio listener, please honestly reevaluate your view and practice of sex and love. I share this story as an extreme and painful example of what I hope will never happen to you. I offer it not as a moral imperative (though it certainly is), but as a message from the heart of God, who wants the very best for you.

> I listened to your radio message this morning. I know from my life's experience that you have spoken truth about the grace of God to break the power of sin. I have suffered from severe sexual immorality. I used it to medicate emotional pain when I was young. Maybe if I tell my story it might be a warning to young people who think being in love justifies sex before marriage.
>
> I was invited to go to a small church by a friend when I was twenty-one years old. That day I saw a girl standing in front of a big oak tree playing with a young girl who attended the church. She was dressed in a white dress, and I loved her when I saw her. I was captured and could not think of anything but her after I saw her. I think maybe once and rarely twice in a lifetime you will meet the person who you will love more than your own life. And Mary was that person in my life.
>
> After pursuing and wooing her for months, I finally got a date. Eventually, one night after taking her out I kissed her for the first time. That kiss left me so weak in the knees. After a while we grew to love each other, and I wish that I could have married her before it went any farther. But we did not realize the consequences of sexual involvement outside of marriage that would eventually destroy me and bring her down into shame. I thought that we would get married soon and that sex was ok. Sex did bond us to each other in ways I didn't understand.
>
> When we traveled together on vacation the next summer, to visit some relatives of mine on a country farm, she asked me to marry her. She felt at home where we were visiting and wanted to

settle down. I told her there was nothing for me in the country and I wanted to return to the city. We could get married then.

Soon after we returned she met another man in college, and eventually I lost her. The emotional pain of that loss was the worst pain I had experienced yet at that point in my life. And to make it worse, I could see her front door from my back window, for I lived on the next street, elevated on a hill that gave me a clear view of her house. She still lived at home with her parents. Because I had caused her to become immoral, she now had a weakness and her new boyfriend exploited it. And I am sure he loved her too. Soon he started staying overnight at her house. That multiplied my emotional pain to know that he was sleeping with her.

So I decided that what I needed was to find someone else to get my mind off the emotional pain. I started looking for any girl that I could use to offset the pain. I would use her and then the next one and the next one. I had no feeling or concern anymore for their emotional welfare. I was driven by a hurt that would never stop hurting. I had lost the only one I would have laid down my life for and now my life was meaningless. I had no hope for a future.

Later I found that going to a strip club seemed to numb me. The incredible beauty of the girls that worked there gave me an anesthetic that delivered me from the pain. They seemed to be so uninhibited and free with their favors that I spent more and more money to get my anesthetic—their attention. I felt that when I went into a club, and by now I had developed dating relationships with some of the dancers, I was free from the only one I ever loved and ruined.

Seven years later, Mary called me and asked me for a loan. She needed to borrow $1,500. I rushed

to meet her and wondered why she would call me.
Surely she would have been married by now. Why
wouldn't her husband meet her needs? I gave her
the money and I noticed that she looked a little
pregnant. She paid me back soon, and she no longer
looked pregnant. When I asked her about her man,
she said that his family had not accepted her,
being that she was white. And he broke off the
relationship after seven years. She made the
comment that she felt like she was married for
a while anyway. I realized that I had funded her
abortion. He had gotten her pregnant and dumped
her. I was angry, hurt, and deeply ashamed because
I felt responsible for her troubles.

A few years later she called me again, needing
$3000 now. She had been caught stealing money from
the company she worked for and they prosecuted
her. She said that if she did not pay it back
they would put her in prison. I met her and said
I would think about it. I was about thirty-two
by now and corrupted by sin and immorality. I had
lost any ability to care for someone in need. And
the one who I would have laid down my life for ten
years ago was in need of mercy and real help. I
eventually told her that if she wanted the money,
she would have to have sex with me one last time.
To my amazement and shame, she agreed.

Somehow in my twisted mind and corrupted heart
and defiled spirit I thought I could rekindle a
long dead relationship. She must have thought
that I was still capable of loving her enough to
be merciful to her in her need. After I succeeded
in lowering her to the level of a prostitute,
she told me soon after that she now felt as if
God had completely left her. We lost touch with
each other and I went back to the nightclub and
strip club life. I did not hear from her again for
another six years. This time she needed me to buy
her some clothes so she could go to an interview.
She had graduated from the Atlanta School of Art

in the photography program. I was so dead and
defiled that she must have seen a mere shadow of
the person I had been fifteen years earlier. But
she had turned a corner. She had recovered a lot
of her beauty. She was living in a hotel room and
looking for an opportunity as a photographer. She
showed me some of her work and I was happy that
she had found something she enjoyed doing. I took
her to a department store and bought clothes for
her and said goodbye.

In 1987 I prayed and told God that if I could
meet a nice girl I would stop destroying myself
and start over. I had held various jobs from
engineering to house remodeling. I met a thirty-
two-year-old Christian woman when I was thirty-
seven. I thought that she was the most wonderful
person I had met in a long time. But because of
the sin I had been caught in for fifteen years
and the total disconnectedness from God that
sin had produced in my life, I had no idea how
to relate to a Christian woman. When I met her,
she was having a Bible study at a Dunkin' Donuts
with a man who worked for me in the construction
business. I sat down and listened and when he
left, I sat there talking to her that whole night
until the next morning. I wondered how she could
have any interest in a person like me. After
several months of seeing her, she and I started
living together—but not in a sexual relationship.
We were more like companions. We did eventually
get involved sexually. She got pregnant, and we
got married.

Truthfully, I really did not love her, but I
did not know it. I thought I did and I wanted a
new life. I thought that God had answered that
desperate prayer. But, you know, she wanted
to meet Mary. I took her to meet Mary when she
was eight months pregnant. She insisted. I was
surprised to even locate Mary. During the visit,
when my wife had gone to the car, I told Mary that

I still wished it could have been her that was
pregnant and that we were married.

My wife eventually realized that I had married
her because I got her pregnant and that I really
could not love her, even though I tried. Her
parents convinced her to divorce me and after two
and a half years she did. We had a house and I was
working for an engineering company and everything
was paid for. I was making good money. I lost
it all in a few months. My wife became the most
bitter and vindictive person from the sweetest and
most trusting person I ever knew. The devastation
from the divorce and the additional two years of
sin I used to try and kill the pain again left
me mentally and spiritually ill and living on
disability for a number of years now. I do have
custody of my daughter, who is now fourteen and a
very gifted girl.

I can still see Mary standing at that oak tree
thirty years ago. Sometimes I drive back to that
church and the tree is still there. I drive back
to the house she lived in when I first kissed her
thirty years ago. I will never be able to love
another person like I loved her. If only I had
married her in honor in that church, how things
would have been different. I would give anything
if I could find her one last time so I could
beg her forgiveness for involving her in sexual
immorality. My mistake destroyed me and brought
her down to shame. The last time I heard about
Mary, she was involved with a married man. I feel
responsible and hope God will allow me to ask her
forgiveness for setting her on the path she is on.

By the grace of God and ten years of unbearable
mental and spiritual suffering from the effects
of long-term sin, I am no longer addicted to
sexual sin. I am completely free from the lust
that took me down to the depths of fornication,
adultery, prostitutes, and financial ruin. I
have lost all my worldly possessions and I am in

some debt. I am doing the best I can to teach my daughter the dangers of sex outside of marriage. She is a believer, but when her mother rejected me, she rejected her daughter also. And her mother emotionally abused my daughter when she was little. I have written this letter to you because although I am free and have experienced God's ability to deliver me from the pit of hell, I still feel defiled and tormented spiritually. I am now fifty-two and I can trace the mess in my life back to sex with the girl I should have known how to love better. Now I hope my story will be a warning to others not to make the same mistake. God doesn't want to take away something good from you; he wants to give you something even better. You said it, Chip—love, sex, and a lasting relationship!

Conclusion

When I read a story like this, it breaks my heart. Lives and love ruined because sex was separated from genuine love. Pain and destruction resulted because God's beautiful gift of sexuality was taken "out of the fireplace" of total commitment in marriage.

All of this raises the $64,000 question: Why has God made marriage so seemingly restrictive? Why would he limit sex to be shared with just one person? How does God's prescription really work?

Personal Evaluation

1. As you read the case studies that were included in this chapter, what feelings or thoughts went through your mind? Why?

2. With which person did you identify the most?

3. From your own experience, how would you explain why knowing the difference between love and sex makes "all the difference"?

4. How do sexual immorality and impurity affect intimacy in a relationship?

5. Why do you think couples who are in a serious "dating relationship" often break up after sex is introduced in the relationship?

7

Why Only One?

God's prescription for lasting relationships asks one man and one woman to enter a relationship of such intimacy and commitment that the two become one for life. He asks us to create a place between two people where sex is celebrated, approved, and enjoyed. Is this even possible? **Why has God designed what seems to be, in our day, such a restrictive pattern as marriage?** Is our hunger for genuine love, vibrant sex, and lasting relationships in the end just a fruitless desire, or will God help us live up to the prescription for marriage that he designed? Or to ask the questions another way, is God being unfairly narrow by expecting monogamy from us or is he actually being profoundly generous by allowing us to have such a relationship as marriage at all? Is marriage designed to restrict and limit our expressions of love or is marriage designed to protect us and vastly deepen our experience of love?

These questions expose our deepest longings and our most painful wounds. After I spoke on the subject of the last chapter recently, a woman approached me and admitted, "I spent the whole time you were talking just trying not to cry." I've heard and read thousands of versions of her statement. You and I are surrounded by people who, when they hear God's prescription for relationships, hang their heads and whisper through tears, "I wish I had known." Perhaps you have the same thoughts. Let me remind you again that the purpose of these chapters is not to weigh you down with guilt but to fill you with enough hope to lighten your load. The same God who lovingly gave a prescription for doing relationships the right way also gave us a prescription for what to do when we do things wrong. Remember, there's hope ahead.

God's Motive for Marriage

The reason God commands us to preserve sex for that one man or one woman in a marriage relationship is **because sexual impurity destroys relationships.** The stories I've heard over the years have gradually shaped the way I look at audiences when I speak about this subject. I now understand that the average person in any group is most likely a person with a shame-filled past. I realize what would happen if such a group could spend several hours during which each person was allowed to tell his or her sexual history anonymously. One by one, their unique accounts would unfold:

> "This is about the first time I had sex."
> "This is how I lost my virginity."
> "This is what happened when I thought I could get love in exchange for sex."
> "This is where I've been."
> "This is what I've done."
> "This is how it broke up my marriage."
> "I remember the first time I had an affair."
> "I remember the first time I logged onto the Internet and found that captivating and explosive world. Let me tell you how my own world unraveled."

Person after person would tell intimate stories from which we would see obvious patterns emerge. The truth would reveal deep hurts. Sex outside God's boundaries destroys people and relationships. The stories would include permanent consequences and pain. Tears would flow in both the telling and the hearing.

"I've got genital herpes and it can't be cured."

"I've got the memory of an abortion I had as a teenager that still gives me nightmares."

"I thought I could bend the rules when I was traveling overseas because I was with strangers, but I brought syphilis home as a painful souvenir."

"I'm HIV positive and ashamed to say I had so many partners I don't know who gave it to me."

"I have AIDS. Let me tell you how I got it."

I'm convinced of this: Before we even open the Bible, the truth we find written in the lives of the average group of fellow human beings would be enough to force us to admit that something is desperately wrong about the way we are doing relationships. Our stories of being hurt, used, and abandoned, thinking this was really love, only to experience the gravest disappointment we've ever experienced—these alone would be enough to convince us! God loves you and me too much for the mess we've created to go on unchallenged. His Word confirms what we know, but it also tells us there's a way out. For those who learn early enough, God's prescription for relationships offers a way around much of the trouble; for those who are already mired in heartache or deadness, God continues to offer hope.

> Sex outside God's boundaries destroys relationships.

Do you know what God wants? He wants you to have a relationship with another person where you look deeply into one another's eyes and you can trust one another. There's no other person in that relationship. There's emotional oneness and there's spiritual oneness. There are adventures, fun, talks, laughter, sex, and if God is willing, even some kids. Throughout life, time and time again you meet each other physically in a celebration of union to the glory of God. You keep the marriage bed holy, and you celebrate sexuality with the approval of God—no guilt, no baggage, not comparing yourself or your mate with any other person. Sex becomes a wholesome, holy, awesome, and mysterious moment in God's presence. God says that the sexual act bonds people's souls like few experiences in the world. He loves you so much that he wants that kind of life for you, for your kids, and for your friends.

But what we see around us is ample evidence that we as a culture have turned away from God's prescription for healthy relationships. Your experience and my experience tell us that sex outside of God's boundaries destroys relationships.

Some Consequences Are for Keeps

All of us know of marriages that are permanently shattered. Many of us know people whose lives include so many twisted and overlapped mistakes, broken relationships, damaged children, that the snag can never be untangled. You and I may sometimes feel like our lives are tied up in knots. I've seen God straighten out situations I thought were hopeless. But I also know that scars remain, even when healing has taken place. I know others who refuse to surrender their messes to God. I've cried with men and women like the man whose story ended the last chapter. His life has been salvaged, but the wreckage left after years of abuse cannot be cleaned up in an instant. Some consequences are for keeps.

After the verses on immorality and greed, the apostle Paul goes on to tell us, "For this you know with certainty, that no immoral or impure person or covetous man, who is an idolater, has an inheritance in the kingdom of Christ and God. Let no one deceive you with empty words, for because of these things the wrath of God comes upon the sons of disobedience" (Eph. 5:5–6 NASB). The Bible reminds us of certain unavoidable certainties.

These verses include a sobering list. It uses the same three characteristics we found earlier (immorality, impurity, and greed) to describe people who will not have "an inheritance in the kingdom of Christ." There's a finality to this statement that gives me chills when I read it.

I realize that it's hard to face our past. It's hard for you and me to own up to our sins. It's difficult to confess what we have intentionally done to others. We hesitate to admit our participation in past activities. We know that if we told our real stories, we would hear others say things like, "Man, think of the people that you've hurt! Think of the families that have been destroyed. Think of the kids that get carted back and forth to different homes." We know we've done wrongs that can't be fixed, even if we are forgiven. When we read verses like the ones above, guilt rears its ugly head and points a bony finger of accusation.

But pay careful attention to what the Bible actually says. Notice that the verses don't address anyone who has ever committed an immoral or impure or greedy *act*. The charge is leveled against the immoral person, the impure person, and the covetous man—it's the idea of someone whose behavior is characterized by these attitudes. If you and I say, "God, I know you have a plan and I know you set some boundaries, but I don't want you or your plan in my life because I'm going to do life my way," then we step right into the sights of these verses. We all stumble, even when we're learning to walk in love, and God's Word warns us. But these verses confront those *who insist on walking their own way*. There's hope for those who stumble, as long as we are trusting in God. That's why, in the verses above, Paul adds a little explanation after the covetous man, pointing out that such people are actually involved in idolatry. Their desires have become their god.

Worship and Sex

The way we use and think of sex ultimately boils down to seeing it either as one of God's gifts or as a means to satisfy selfish ends. Sex outside of God's ideal of marriage—the lusting, taking,

"I've got to have it" using of people—blatantly disregards God. Interestingly enough, the ancients had one thing right—there is a connection between sex and worship. But they made a huge mistake when they applied the truth. They worshipped sex instead of God who gave it. Instead of recognizing sex as one of the wonderful things about creation that point to the Creator, they made part of the creation into an idol to be worshipped by misusing the gift. Our culture has made the same mistake. At the heart of sexual immorality lies an attitude of worship, but it's worship of a terribly wrong kind. In sexual immorality we worship ourselves at the expense of others. Ultimately, sexual immorality is worship of my needs, my rights, my lust, and me. It's not love.

How do sex and worship connect in God's prescription? The answer lies in the verses we looked at in the last chapter. The Bible uses an attitude of thanksgiving to contrast with the immoral, impure, and greedy person. Genuine worship has much to do with gratitude. When God describes the deepest problems of the human condition, he certainly says we have all sinned (Rom. 3:23). He also points out that we have forgotten to give thanks (Rom. 1:21). If God has given us such a gift as sexuality, then our truest form of gratefulness will be shown by the way we handle the gift. The relationship of marriage provides the only God-designed setting in which a man and a woman can express deep gratitude to their Creator as they share his gift of sexuality with each other for life. The fact that this sounds strange to our ears simply indicates how deeply ingrained the self-centered Hollywood formula has become in our thinking. A view of love that has no place for God will produce neither love nor gratitude to God for his generosity.

The Danger of Empty Words

Notice that the verses go on to say, ***"Let no one deceive you with empty words"*** (Eph. 5:6 NASB). Another translation says, ***"Don't be fooled by those who try to excuse these sins"*** (NLT). When it comes to sexuality, the world is full of empty words, like when we give kids false slogans such as "safe sex" or "recreational sex" or when we change terms or substitute expressions to avoid the truth as with "it's just an affair" or "fling." But adultery under any empty name is still adultery. Changing the terminology may temporarily stifle the truth, but it doesn't change it. Adultery is still a multiple betrayal of self and others. If we've made a vow (given our word) before God, before our partner, and before other witnesses, and then betrayed our promises, we've committed adultery. It's not a casual "affair"; it's sin, and it sets into motion a sequence of devastating effects.

You see, sexual impurity (inside or outside marriage) destroys relationships. The first relationship we learn that it destroys is the one with God. People who progressively continue in sexual immorality are really saying, "I'm going to worship me." And that means we don't worship God. I find people are actually shocked to discover that fact. When we relegate God to a little corner of our life and instruct him to wait quietly until we get around to giving him attention, it's not surprising that when we do turn to him, we find him missing. Worship is exclusive. That means we can't worship or serve more than one god. We can't make life all about us and then expect God to fall in line. Sin breaks fellowship.

Remember the last time you knowingly violated some part of God's prescription for living? Perhaps nothing bad happened immediately. You may have even concluded you had a lot of fun. But how was your prayer life after that? Did you find it possible to have deep intimacy with God in your prayer life after you had been involved with sexual sin? Did you feel close to God? See him answering prayers on a regular basis? Or did you feel condemned, dirty, and ashamed? Did you find yourself eating, shopping, or returning to the same sin to avoid the feelings? Did you find yourself restless, turning music up louder, suddenly uncomfortable being alone? The boundaries in God's prescription are not there because God is a prude but because he loves you so much. God knows that sexual impurity will destroy your relationship with him.

But please hear this added note. The God who made us understood that you and I would struggle. When Jesus died on the cross, he paid for your sins and mine—all of them. The immoral, impure, and covetous person stays that way because they refuse God's remedy. We can't work or wish our way out of our problem. But God has already arranged for the load, the guilt, and the baggage of your past to be lifted. Jesus already handled it. No matter what your past, you can stop today and say, "Lord Jesus, I've been doing sexual life my way, and it's destroyed my relationship with you and with other people. Would you forgive me?" Know what you'll find? Once you open your heart and get honest with God, you won't find a God with his arms crossed, his finger pointed at you, and his toe tapping, saying, "Well, I was wondering when you were going to come around because, boy, am I mad at you." Instead, you're going to meet a God whose heart is broken, who will gaze at you through tears of compassion and say, "You've been destroying yourself. I knew this would happen; I sent my Son to solve this. I sent my Son to pay your debt and to break the power of sin in your life. You can start over. You can do relationships my way. You can have intimacy, you can be loved, you can be cherished, you can realize your wife or husband is not an object but a life partner. Today we can draw a line in the sand; you can receive forgiveness for your past, and then start a journey toward the future." We need these words of hope.

> God knows that sexual impurity will destroy your relationship with him.

Sexual impurity not only destroys our relationship with God, it also destroys our relationships with others. We've already seen the heartache, confusion, and betrayal caused by sexual impurity in the stories we've read. Those who try to practice sex and love in these ways are basing life on empty words. They are headed toward destruction, because some consequences are unavoidable.

The final phrase in the verses we read earlier is **"because of these things the wrath of God comes upon the sons of disobedience"** (Eph. 5:6 NASB). The wrath of God (his anger) describes the consequences of disobeying and disregarding God's prescription. We don't think often or clearly enough about God's wrath.

God hates evil. It makes him angry with a holy and just anger. The closest we human beings come to this kind of anger is when we witness the suffering of a little one. Watching a small child beaten or abused instantly sparks a wave of righteous anger in us. We would be driven to intervene—violently if necessary. When obvious evil occurs, the fact that you are made in the image of God also makes you capable of righteous anger. Why? Because something you love is being harmed or destroyed.

God made this planet, he made you, he made sexuality, he made marriage. Whenever we do something that violates what he made, he gets very, very angry. Why? Because sin destroys his relationship with you. It destroys your relationship with others. Sin is not loving, and it destroys you and me. Sin makes God mad. Jesus, when he died on the cross, absorbed the just wrath of God, so now genuine forgiveness is available. But in this fallen world consequences are one way God reminds us of the depth and reality of evil. Consequences can cause us, after a while, to say, "Maybe God's Word is right. Maybe I should do it his way." I know that some of us are very hardheaded, so consequences take effect on us more slowly. We may have to hit our head against the wall three or four times before we pay attention. And we go through multiple relationships or even marriages before stopping to think seriously. It may take a sexually transmitted disease or desperate loneliness to bring us to the place where we say, "God, I'm sorry. Your way is right."

Getting Our Attention

I remember developing a friendship with a fellow player on an outreach basketball team a number of years ago. We traveled and played together throughout South America. Most of the players were great players from big-name schools. We competed against amateur and professional teams, sharing our faith during the extended halftimes of the games. I quickly discovered that my new friend usually spent his summers playing professional baseball in the minor leagues. During the year he attended a major university, where he was a varsity basketball player.

Traveling on this Christian team, we ended up rooming together. We hit it off great. Along with his athletic skills, he was an easy-going, great-looking guy who seemed to be enjoying the experience. When we started sharing our spiritual journey, he surprised me with his vulnerability. He said, "You know, it's so good to be part of this. Most summers I'm busy playing pro ball." Then he added thoughtfully, "Finally, God got my attention."

"What do you mean?" I asked.

He said, "Well, I guess the best way to describe it is that I've been an idolater. I've spent all my life so far worshipping me. I never saw it that way before, but a few months ago I realized it's what I have been." I wasn't sure how to respond. After a few moments he realized a little more explanation would probably be helpful.

"When I began playing on the road," he continued, "I got a real buzz from the crowd and I discovered I was attractive to ladies." He shook his head as if remembering something painful. "You know, as we moved from town to town all over America, there were times I had sex multiple times a day with different women. They threw themselves at us after the games. And then at school, as a big basketball star, sex was a perk. At first, it was the game outside the game—how often and with how many different co-eds could I have sex? I lost count of the number. My life revolved around sex." There wasn't a hint of bragging in his voice. The words came from him slowly and shamefully, like terrible weights he wanted to drop.

"I went through about three years of this. Then I woke up one day and I was numb." He stopped for a moment, allowing me to absorb the significance of his confession. "I didn't feel anything. I didn't know who I was anymore. I didn't know how to have a relationship. I was like someone who stuck his hand in a fire over and over. The first few times, the jolts were memorable. But once the hand got burned enough and the nerves died under the ugly scars, the hand stopped feeling. My body actually came to the point that it didn't respond. I was a sexual burnout. My heart got dull, my brain wouldn't respond." I will never forget the tone of deep sadness and loss in his voice as he murmured, "There's a tiny piece torn from me that I left with each of these women that I can never get back." He described his years of indulgence in selfish sex by comparing it to being a piece of cardboard. Every time he had sex he was being glued to another piece of cardboard just long enough for the glue to dry. When the pieces were pulled apart, neither piece of cardboard came away whole.

"There are pieces of me all over with these women everywhere," he said. "I don't even know who I am, and I don't know how to have a relationship." Then he concluded with a sob, "I got to where I didn't enjoy sex and I didn't like me. I was so far from God that I knew I was lost. Getting invited on this trip was God's gracious answer to my cry for help. As we go from country to country, I'm also on a spiritual journey. I'm asking God little by little to heal me."

There probably isn't one man reading the first part of the account above who at least once in some weak moment didn't think, "Now that would be the life! Unlimited access to women." But the consequences in this story overwhelm the earlier excitement and motivation. Idolatry, as my friend discovered, exacts a very heavy cost. In his case, several years of indulging will lead to a lifetime of regrets. But if you identify painfully with his experience, don't miss the grace of God in his life. He was finding healing. He was discovering, little by little, God's good purposes even in his wrath. God loves you and me so much that he wants us to know that when we ignore his prescription and take our sexuality outside the box of one woman or one man for all time, it eventually will destroy our relationships with other people, it will destroy our relationship with God, and, ultimately, as with my friend, it will destroy our relationship with ourselves.

Where Do We Go from Here?

Let me repeat the recurring theme of hope that God wants you to remember. I told you the story above because it is such a powerful example of how consequences swallow up the pleasures of immorality but also of how hope and grace cover a multitude of sins. Wherever you find yourself today, there's hope for you within God's mercy and grace.

In the next chapter I want to address a subject that is important to all of us. Whether you are a young, single person struggling to clarify God's prescription for love, sex, and lasting relationships so that you can pursue life confidently or a wounded traveler who has a collection of consequences through which you have come to seek God's help, all of us need to have an understanding of how to maintain sexual purity in a sex-saturated society. If we are going to avoid relational mistakes the first time or avoid making the same mistakes again, we need to have a clear picture of God's provision and power for sexual purity.

> Wherever you find yourself today, there's hope for you within God's mercy and grace.

In a word, what we've said in this chapter is that *God wants you to walk in love.* Relationships, loving other people, and this intimate fellowship that comes out of the soil of love takes time, energy, and commitment. And there are clear boundaries. That's why God designed us for marital relationship with one person. God longs for you to have a relationship with the opposite sex that is so rich and wonderful that when you celebrate sex, it will be a holy, mysterious, awesome moment both in the sight of God and in your experience.

Before we look at *how* to maintain sexual purity, I'm going to ask you to make a decision about your sexuality and your relationships. I ask you to accept God's boundless love for you. The decision to accept God's design for genuine love means you must commit yourself (or recommit yourself) to his standard of purity in applying his prescription for love, sex, and lasting relationships. This is a commitment to be sexually pure in thought, word, and deed.

First, a specific invitation to *uninvolved singles*, and by uninvolved I mean you're not in a relationship right now. I'd like you to make a decision that you will develop personal convictions about sexual purity. Draw a line in the sand and declare, "I will do relationships this way. I will not have sex before I'm married. I will not get involved beyond this level physically before I get married. I won't settle for second best." Make a decision today, before you read the next chapter. Then ask God for the grace to live out that commitment daily.

Second, a word to the *involved,* by which I mean that you're in a relationship that you know needs a clearer understanding of God's prescription. I'd like you to make a decision to have an honest conversation in the next few days to evaluate your relationship with regard to sexual purity. If you are going too far sexually, stop the behavior and set new boundaries. (The next chapter will help you.) If you are living together, determine to move apart in order to do this relationship God's way. You'll never regret it.

Third, a word to those *in crisis.* Perhaps one of the following statements describes the state of your relationship:

If the truth were known, your marriage is just about to break up.

You have an addiction problem with sex and pornography.

You've become a habitual user of sexual Internet sites.

You've considered unfaithfulness or have been unfaithful.

You find yourself with homosexual fantasies or are involved in a homosexual relationship.

You find yourself drawn to children or you find yourself in some other perversion.

These problems pervade every level and corner of society. They are as present in the church as they are in seedy neighborhoods. If this chapter revealed you have open raw wounds, you may need immediate professional help. Don't hesitate. Help is available to those willing to seek it. I can tell you this: The hole you are hiding in isn't so deep that God's grace can't reach and pull you out. Go to a pastor, a professional counselor, or a group designed for those with sexual addictions.

Finally, let me add a word of hope for all of us. I imagine that as you've read this chapter, some pictures probably came to mind of people you've hurt or times that you have been hurt, and you really wonder, "Can God forgive all that junk, all that trash, all that stuff?" I'll let God speak for himself:

> "Come now, let us reason together,"
>   says the LORD.
> "Though your sins are like scarlet,
>   they shall be as white as snow;
> though they are red as crimson,
>   they shall be like wool."
>
>   Isaiah 1:18

Would you like that? Would you like to know that all your sexual past, all the people you've hurt, all the things you've been through, all the things you've done, said, thought of—all of that can be gone? Today, you can bow your head and pray the following words: "God, these stories and your Word are revealing things about me that may only be the tip of the iceberg. I can already see specific mistakes and sins that I have committed. You know all this, but I want to name them in your presence as a specific act of confession on my part. Lord, I have . . . [personalize what God's Spirit has shown you]. I now recognize these as intentional or unintentional sins that I have committed against you, even as I have harmed others and myself. Will you please forgive me on the basis of what Jesus did on the cross, will you cleanse me, will you help me live for you from this day forward?"

He will. God will reinstate his prescription for relationships in your life, starting with his relationship with you. You can delay or turn away, but the cost will be heavy. God has something in mind for you that is so much better, you can hardly imagine it. God's plan for you, whether you're married, single, or about to be married, unless he gives you the gift of singleness, is to be in a warm, loving marriage relationship, characterized by open communication, a lot of hard work, deep commitment, setting boundaries, and doing it God's way. There will be times when you go back to the bedroom, and as a celebration of who God is and in thankfulness for his gifts you share, you will enjoy the best sex known on this planet—guilt-free, baggage-free, Holy Spirit–inspired, as an act of grateful worship to your heavenly Father. That's what God thinks about sex and love. It flows out of the purity and the protective boundaries he has provided for us.

If you think it is just impossible to live a sexually pure life in a sex-saturated world or you simply don't know how, stay with me for the next chapter.

Personal Evaluation

1. How does God's command concerning monogamy reveal his love for us?

2. What is the connection between worship and sex?

3. Why do you think people today still get confused about the connection between worship and sex?

4. In what ways did you find the closing story about the basketball player a source of hope for you and your relationships?

5. What specific step(s) do you need to take in response to what you learned in this chapter:

   a. Make a commitment to sexual purity?
   b. Have a talk to set boundaries with your boyfriend/ girlfriend?
   c. Get help in your struggles with a sexual addiction?
   d. Other _____

8

How to Say Yes to Love and No to Second-Rate Sex

The question arched through the air toward me like a large piece of ripe fruit, and those watching expected me to get a face-full of pulp. I was sitting on the floor in a dorm room on a college campus surrounded by six or seven young men. The topic under discussion was sexual purity, and the tension in the room was almost palpable. Although a couple of the fellows were Christians and clearly rooting for me, it was definitely a hostile environment when it came to anything the Bible had to say about sex.

One of them finally asked a question that was on all their minds and which most of them believed was unanswerable. It was one of those questions that often stumped me as a young Christian. But on this particular occasion I was ready for it. The young man, obviously the leader in the group, leaned forward and said, "You Christians always use the Bible to answer questions. I'm not sure

I can trust it. So without quoting the Bible, can you give me a good reason why I should save sex for marriage?"

There was a moment of awkward silence. The group looked pleased that someone had voiced their frustration. The two Christian young men were certainly hoping I would come up with something good; the others seemed to think I was pinned against the wall. With a short, grateful prayer to God for what he'd taught me in the past, I said, "I'll make a deal with all of you. Will you listen to what the Bible says about saving sex for marriage if I give you not one but *five* good reasons for saving sex for marriage that aren't in the Bible?"

My response certainly caught them by surprise. They looked at each other with a mixture of confusion and curiosity. When they looked back at me in cautious agreement, I knew that if I gave them five good reasons not to have sex until marriage, they would at least let me present what the Bible has to say concerning love, sex, and lasting relationships.

The scenario I described above represents scores of conversations I've had over the last twenty years with college students. Although I can't remember the details of each situation, the mood, the questions, and the issues have remained the same. When it comes to love, the hunger for direction and truth lies hidden just beneath the surface in most people's lives. Summarized below are the five reasons that I've given in countless settings. They are not based on biblical passages but on scientific research.

Five Facts about Sex

Here are five significant facts about sexual purity that I have gleaned from published reports:

1. Those who abstain from sexual intercourse before marriage report the highest levels of sexual satisfaction in marriage. In fact, those who report they are very sexually satisfied in their lives are not good-looking singles who have multiple partners and who go barhopping to find the right

person at the right time for this exciting life. Research done by Bethesda Research Group reported in the *Washington Post* in 1994 concluded, **"Couples who strongly believe that sex outside of marriage is wrong are a whopping 31 percent more satisfied in their sex lives."**[1]

2. "Those who cohabitate or live together before marriage have a 50 percent higher possibility of divorce than those who do not."[2] Researchers at UCLA discovered that not only do those who cohabitate have a higher level of divorce, they are more likely to commit adultery once they get married.

3. By contrast, the University of South Carolina in a study said that those who abstain from sexual intercourse before marriage have the highest rates of marital fidelity.[3]

4. **"The introduction of sex in a dating relationship is almost always the ushering in of the breakup of that relationship."**[4] Doctors Les and Leslie Parrott made this statement after interviewing thousands of single people on college campuses. We discussed this earlier.

5. "Sexually transmitted diseases, including AIDS, can remain dormant, asymptomatic (you don't know you have it), for up to a decade or more, but be passed on to others during that time."[5] The rampant spread of STDs flatly contradicts those who try to claim that sexual intercourse is a harmless recreational activity to be pursued with the largest number of partners possible. People are paying with their lives and their health for accepting that lie.

As you can see above, the more persistent our attempts to carry out the Hollywood formula, the more abundant the evidence is that the plan doesn't work. The scientific research over the past few decades makes it overwhelmingly clear that God's prescription really is in our best interests. Further, the results of the research back the biblical teaching at every turn. Yet even though this data is published in widely distributed media, it seems to have little effect. Why? Because the volume of Hollywood's messages drowns out common sense. What makes me sad when I look at the facts above is that they present such devastating evidence of wreckage in people's lives. By the time they become statistics, too many people are suffering from errors that could be avoided. That's why God's prescription has such value; it presents a way of living that anticipates the struggles and the temptations. It gives us a way through the minefield of problems and mistakes we will stumble into if we try to figure life out as we go along. I'm hoping that, like the young people in the group I mentioned above, you are ready to give serious consideration to what the Bible says about relationships. There are two important facts you must understand about sex in God's prescription.

Fact 1. Loving Relationships Demand Sexual Purity

I haven't stated this truth this plainly before, but loving relationships demand sexual purity. I'm amazed how easy it is to fall into the mindset that assumes we can plant the seeds of sexual impurity and expect to reap a harvest of loving relationships. My athlete friend's story from the end of the last chapter demonstrated how devastating it can be to reap a harvest of emotional deadness after a few years of self-indulgent behavior. If all the patterns in creation tell us that we reap what we sow, then we probably should conclude that if we really want to reap loving relationships, we should plant the seeds that produce those results—and those seeds are sexual purity.

Walking in Love

All the research I just quoted confirms the kind of relational harvest we see in people's lives every day. If we plant seeds of wanton lust, or seeds of using and abusing people, or seeds of indiscriminate sex and self-centered pleasure, we should not be surprised by the fields of toxic weeds that cover our lives. But if we want the harvest of a loving, deep, intimate relationship, we need to understand that a loving relationship demands sexual purity. It's not optional. This truth underlies everything we've said so far.

When we examined Ephesians 5:2–4 and what it means to "walk in love," we could have included sexual purity as one of the prime illustrations of how we accomplish that kind of living. When we walk in love, we really love people. That includes actions you take and actions you save for the right time. When you really love people, not just lust for them, you do what is best for them. You make sacrifices. You are selfless. You are a giver. You care about them and what they get instead of what you want. When you do that, you are following Christ's example.

By contrast, loving is not just positive action. If you really love someone, you choose not to do certain things, because to do them would be destructive or would ruin the relationship. Our discussion of immorality, impurity, and greed (Eph. 5:3–4) delved into the many ways our culture fosters the very kinds of relational behavior that are self-destructive and produce dysfunctional relationships.

In short, God is all for sex, in the context of sexual purity. I've met plenty of people (I used to be one of them) who ask, "Where does the Bible say sex outside of marriage is wrong?" This question doesn't reveal that it's hard to find what the Bible says about sex; it reveals the person hasn't read the Bible. God's prescription is taught and illustrated everywhere in the Bible. It doesn't get any clearer. Sex outside of marriage is wrong. It's not wrong because God is a prude. It's not wrong because sex is bad. It's wrong because a loving relationship demands sexual purity. Genuine love is giving, and illicit sex has to do with lusting and getting. Great sex is actually a result of sexual purity—check the research!

God protects intimacy and sex within the shelter of a marriage commitment as a reflection of his holiness and love. He built into life certain consequences that flow as a result of unloving, selfish, destructive behavior, in order to get people's attention and offer them a way back. That's why there are diseases. That's why people break up. That's why when you live together before you're married, your sexual satisfaction goes down and the divorce rate goes up. God loves you so much that there are consequences to doing things outside of his will—for your ultimate good.

Some people say, "I'm going to stiff-arm God. I don't want a loving relationship if the price tag includes sexual purity. I want what I want. And I want to be fulfilled no matter what or who it hurts!" Well, God's Word promises consequences, the final one being that terrible judgment we read in Ephesians 5:5: "Okay. No inheritance in the kingdom of God" (my paraphrase). The invitation to "walk in love," as much as it has to do with our relationships with other people, has even more to do with our relationship with God. Alongside the command to "walk in love" (Eph. 5:2), we also find the command to "walk in the light" (Eph. 5:8).

Walking in Light

After telling the Ephesians about the importance of "walking in love" and the consequences of not doing so, the apostle Paul returned to the practical question of God's prescription for living and loving in Ephesians 5:7–10.

> Therefore do not be partakers with them; for you were formerly darkness, but now you are Light in the Lord; walk as children of Light (for the fruit of the Light consists in all goodness and righteousness and truth), trying to learn what is pleasing to the Lord. [NASB]

"Once you see that the world isn't walking in love," says Paul, "don't participate in their way of living." In other words, don't be a partner. Don't associate. Don't be connected. Don't live anymore the way you used to live. Don't think like they think or watch what they watch. Don't view sex the same way they do. Don't court fantasies about sex like they do. Why? The next phrase answers the inevitable question. "For you were formerly darkness, but now you are Light in the Lord." This isn't about laws and rules—it's about new living. The Bible consistently describes the world's view as darkness. Once we've welcomed the light, we can't live in darkness anymore.

I remember darkness. I remember the hopelessness and despair of living for little more than myself. I know what it did to my relationships. I know that you know what it has done to your relationships. We were darkness. But once you and I come to know Christ, our past is forever put behind us. I'm forgiven and you're forgiven (or you can be, if you have not yet acknowledged Christ for who he is). When we do accept Christ, repent of our sin, and receive forgiveness, the Spirit of God comes into our lives. We're adopted into God's family. We are "children of Light." We've been changed. We are compelled by this new life within us to live a new and better way—God's way.

You may ask, "What does walking in the light look like?" I guess God knew we would ask that question, so he provided a clear answer in Ephesians 5:9. There are three kinds of fruit or evidences of walking in the light—goodness, righteousness, and truth. Let me define those words to help you picture yourself as a child of God walking in the light while living in a sex-saturated culture.

The word **goodness** has to do with personal character. Goodness is love in action. It's the achievement of moral excellence combined with a generous spirit. You become the kind of person who isn't trying to take, get, or manipulate. Instead, you're the kind of person who wants to give, bless, and encourage.

The word **righteousness** was used in ancient Greek culture to describe someone who gives to each person what he or she is justly due, in relation to God and to man. Righteousness in our lives comes out in fairness, justice, and care for others. We know what's right to do and we do it. There's no hidden agenda.

Truth is a beautiful word that merits our continuous meditation. It includes the idea of practicing integrity and bringing beauty to relationships. Truth involves honesty, purity, winsomeness, and wholeness. The apostle was saying, "As children of the light, carry out relationships in such a way that you give out good instead of trying to manipulate and get. Recognize what's right to do and do it! And build relationships where there's truth and beauty and intimacy—relationships that are not based on games but on God and his prescription for loving."

These two phrases picture God's dream for you—**walking in love** and **walking in light.** The fact that these phrases are foreign to our relational vocabulary is evidence of the darkness that still infiltrates our lives and culture. We tolerate this stuff about having multiple partners. This stuff about trying to find someone through sexual attraction. This stuff about hooking up and playing the game to find out how far you can go. This stuff about having a routine marriage and being secretly hooked on pornography, telling dirty jokes, or being adept at innuendo. These clouds of darkness pollute and mask the majesty, the awe, and the beauty of what God designed for you and me. He wants something so much better for you. His dream features loving relationships, which demand sexual purity.

Sexual purity in this sex-saturated world may seem impossible to you. Well, I'm about to tell you that it's not only possible; the rewards are phenomenal. So what does it take to break out of the sex-saturated patterns of our culture? It takes a carefully crafted game plan. This brings us to the second fact about sex in God's prescription.

Fact 2. Sexual Purity Demands a Game Plan

So far we've looked at five solid reasons why sex before marriage, even apart from the scriptural evidence, is a very poor decision. As we've noted, God's plan demonstrates its wisdom by predicting what the scientific research confirms. In other words, you can expect certain results if you follow God's prescription:

- If you stay sexually pure, then you can expect to have better sex in your marriage.
- If you stay sexually pure, then you can expect the possibility of divorce to go down by 50 percent.

- If you stay sexually pure, then you can expect your relationship to last.
- If you stay sexually pure, then you can expect to avoid the sexually transmitted diseases that are destroying so many lives.
- If you stay sexually pure and accept someone as a potential mate who lives by the same values, then you can expect that when you marry, each of you will remain faithful to the other.

But if you stopped here, you would face a huge problem. You will fail if you walk into the world armed with only *intellectual* facts about why God's prescription is a more logical and practical approach to love, sex, and lasting relationships. Unfortunately, we do not make decisions based solely on our intellectual knowledge or logical processes, particularly when our hormones are involved. You need much more than facts.

We humans are emotional beings who make some of our most important decisions on impulses and peer pressure. Think for a moment about the thousands of people who know about the proven dangers of smoking, drinking while driving, and overeating but whose actions directly contradict their knowledge of the facts. This same principle applies in the way we handle our sexuality. Facts will not be enough to control our actions.

I could make an educated guess that if you closed this book right now, within the next twenty-four hours you would suffer some major setbacks in trying to implement God's prescription in your life, even if you fully resolved to do so. Between your habits and our culture's traps, you're an easy target. Before the day is done, you may watch a football game or other sporting event that will include enough commercials with innuendos and messages that will plant subliminal thoughts in your mind like these: "If I only had this kind of beer, or this kind of car, or that kind of deodorant, beautiful gorgeous women would be falling at my feet." Or, if you're a member of the fairer sex, the unconscious message would be, "If I start using that certain kind of margarine, or wearing that secret lingerie, some handsome hunk with wavy hair and bulging biceps will appear in my living room and announce, 'Baby! I can't believe it's butter, and I can't believe it's you!'"

I'm jesting, but the point is that you and I are inundated with promotions for Hollywood's sexual formula. Life is filled with lethal traps that we stumble into because of the things we hear and see all the time. Yes, you need to have good and powerful reasons to live by God's prescription. You need to trust in his help. But you also need something more: **You need a game plan!**

Without a game plan, maintaining sexual purity is a pipe dream. If your honest desire is to live a sexually pure life for all the reasons mentioned above and most importantly to please God and prepare yourself for the best love, sex, and lasting relationship, there's hope. Below are four specific steps you can take to develop a game (or battle) plan for living life God's way in the arena of your sexuality.

Step 1. Develop Convictions

The first step is to develop convictions. **Purity requires a personal commitment to the truth.** The particular truth I'm talking about is verses 2–4 of Ephesians 5. The truth forbids sex of any kind that is outside God's ordained design of one man and one woman within the marriage commitment. Say with your heart and mind, "I'm not going there. I'm not going to go there mentally. I'm not going to go there in my speech. I'm not going to go there in my lifestyle." This makes it a **personal commitment, a conviction that will affect your choices.** I don't mean intellectually agreeing with what the Bible says or what research has revealed. I don't mean adopting the beliefs of others you admire. I'm talking about a personal conviction where you own a certain standard. From your heart, you say, "I am willfully going to make a personal commitment to live a life where my mind will be sexually pure, my speech will be sexually pure, and my actions will be sexually pure. I'm going to do it God's way, whether I'm married or single."

I realize many of you may still be wondering, "What's the difference between intellectually believing in something and having a conviction?" Let me give you a picture. As a brand-new Christian in my early college days, I was instructed to read the Bible. I got through the New Testament a few times but usually got lost in the Old Testament. I was in some Bible studies, but our discussions were pretty lightweight—just about what I could handle.

I was in a school that gave me financial help in exchange for my athletic participation and other duties to be decided along the way. As part of my room and board payment, I was designated a Resident Assistant and put in charge of a floor in the dorm. Part of the training for this role involved a seminar in values clarification, which was popular in the 1970s. Much of it was mundane and commonsense details. But one group exercise altered my life forever. The leaders gathered us together in the center of a large room, with a line marked on the floor from one end to the other. One of them explained that we were about to answer some significant questions—physically. The line on the floor was a continuum, with one end representing complete agreement with a statement and the other end complete disagreement with a statement. After each statement was read, we were to walk to the place on the floor that most clearly represented what we believed.

> Purity requires a personal commitment to the truth.

I knew most of the other students in the group and two of them, Dana and Jana, were part of a Bible study I attended. The facilitator said, "Here's the first statement: *Premarital sex is wrong.* Those who agree, move toward the right; those who disagree, move to the left." Of the seventy students in the room, sixty-seven en masse walked to the far left side, declaring by their action (and numerous audible comments), "We totally disagree with that." This was, after all, a decade when the sexual revolution was raging. Dana and Jana walked to the far right, unconditionally agreeing with the statement. One guy walked in Dana and Jana's direction, about two steps to the right of the middle of the line. That guy was me.

I had a problem. I was willing to move a little in the right direction, but I wasn't committed and I wasn't definite. I had an intellectual belief that sex before marriage is wrong, but my conviction wasn't fully developed. I didn't believe to the point of openly acting on that belief 100 percent of the time. There's nothing like social pressure or peer pressure to demonstrate the strength of our convictions (or lack of them).

I had been a Christian for a couple of years and had been raised in a pretty good moral home. I thought I knew where I stood—until it came time to stand there! I looked across the floor at the sixty-seven people who were saying, "Are you nuts? Get a life! Coed dorms are the way to go. Free love is the answer." In their stares I could hear, "Do you really believe this?" And over half of them were girls—three or four of whom I was interested in. See the difference? I unhappily demonstrated my partial belief system. Dana and Jana demonstrated their conviction.

What do you have when it comes to sexual purity—an optional belief system or rock-solid convictions? When you close this book and turn on the television or go on your next date, how will your actions demonstrate what you really believe? How does what you say you believe affect what you do with sexual urges? In what ways do you demonstrate convictions when you get on the Internet or walk by the convenience store and notice all those magazines? What happens to your convictions when you flip on the television and some sensual scene from a soap opera comes on and you know it's the antithesis of everything you believe about godly love? Do you get sucked in or express your convictions with the remote? Do you have a conviction before God that says, "I'm going to switch the station immediately, not because someone else is watching but because I'm convinced that God loves me so much that he allowed Jesus to die on the cross for me to deliver me from self-destructive behavior. He cares for me so much that I'm going to do life his way. Not because of anyone or anything else. This is between God and me—no matter what responses or repercussions I get from others. I'm going to do life God's way." That's a conviction.

Step 2. Ponder the Consequences

The second step of God's game plan is to ponder the consequences of sexual sin. Ephesians 5:5–6 lists some heavy consequences. People who do life, relationships, and sexual activity outside the boundaries of God's way eventually will experience the wrath of God. Pondering consequences can provoke a certain amount of fear, and that's okay. Fear can be a legitimate and healthy motivation for delayed gratification.

We need to ponder carefully the spiritual price tag of not doing life God's way when we are tempted to indulge in sexual fantasies or sexual behavior. We need to remember the feelings of guilt and shame that always follow sexual sin and what it does to our relationship with God. We must force ourselves to calculate the relational price tag of what it will do to the person we're involved with or our mate or our children. You would be amazed at what a powerful deterrent it is to imagine a lifetime with AIDS or genital herpes in exchange for a few moments of pleasure. Or consider the financial price tag when you discover your girlfriend is pregnant, or when your uncontrolled passion results in a broken home and you are paying for a divorce, childcare, and alimony.

I find pondering the consequences very healthy. When I'm facing the kinds of temptations I know you face too, this is what I do. I picture in my mind calling a family conference and lining up on the couch our four kids, with my wife sitting in tears on the far side of the room. I imagine trying to tell them how, after all the things I've preached about the past twenty-five years, I blew it. I cringe as I think of the look in my daughter's eyes as I tell her I betrayed her and her mother, or the look in my sons' eyes if I tell them I've been involved in pornography after all the conversations we've had about its dangers. Then, after allowing my mind to play out these painful scenes of consequences, I imagine standing before an audience of people who have trusted me and shared their lives with me, and I hear myself confessing my failure. I see the disappointment, anger, sadness, and loss in their faces. I hear the whispers, "See, the whole thing's a sham. He preached it, but he didn't live it."

This pondering about the consequences has to be vivid and honest. It has to remove any sense of confidence in ourselves and our ability to stay true to God's plan on our own. The Bible warns, "If you think you are standing strong, be careful, for you, too, may fall into the same sin" (1 Cor. 10:12 NLT). Pondering consequences will create a healthy sense of fear and drive you to God—and it ought to.

If all this sounds too dramatic, consider the testimony of Scripture. Reading about King David, a "man after God's own heart" who failed morally, reminds me that all of us are vulnerable. I remember studying the passage about David's adultery with Bathsheba and writing in the margin of my Bible, "Not a bad man, but a good man in a weak moment." The Scripture is clear: Any good man or good woman, in a weak moment, in certain circumstances, can go over the edge morally. What that tells me is that a good, healthy dose of fear is needed to back up my intentions. The writer of the Proverbs tells us, "The fear of the LORD is the beginning of wisdom" (9:10a). Wisdom is not merely intellectual acumen. Wisdom is the skill and understanding to do life God's way—to experience God's blessing and favor.

Step 3. Pre-decide Your Actions

The third step of the game plan is to make pre-decisions. **Advanced decision making is absolutely essential for sexual purity.** Ephesians 5:7–9 tells us to walk as children of the light. There are certain areas in our spiritual lives that require us to "stand firm" and do battle with the enemy (see Eph. 6:10–17), but there are certain areas in our spiritual lives that require us to flee.

Second Timothy 2:22 describes what fleeing means: "Run from anything that gives you the lustful thoughts that young men often have. But stay close to anything that makes you want to do right. And enjoy the companionship and love of those who want to honor God and walk with him in holiness" (TLB). The idea here is to escape youthful lust. It's not about being strong; it's about knowing when to retreat. Imagine being with your girlfriend or boyfriend at 2:30 in the morning, downstairs on the couch lying prone. You rationalize, *We're watching a movie.* But you have impulses and hormones that don't obey rational thought. You care deeply for one another, and you think you never would go beyond what you're doing now. But as long as you stay in that tempting environment, you are actually facilitating your failure—not because you're weaklings, not because you're dumb, and not because you lack commitment, but because you're in a tempting situation and you don't have the strength to resist it.

The parallels apply whether we're talking about the "innocent" lunch with a fascinating coworker or the casual visits to a semi-pornographic site on the Internet. Putting ourselves in these situations is like embracing fire and then wondering why we got badly burned. You and I are not strong enough for many temptations. No one is. The key to our response is advance decisions. Let me give you a few examples.

When dirty jokes start at work or school. I remember being in the teachers' lounge when I taught school. They would start with the dirty stuff, and I would say I had to go. At other times I would say, "Hey guys, I don't think this is appropriate." Advance decision making.

When something comes on TV that is offensive or suggestive. If a show is on and people start taking off their clothes and you feel yourself being drawn in, use the remote in your hand and [beep] it's gone. Don't say, "Oh, my. This is disgraceful. I can't believe this is on at prime time. The children in America shouldn't be watching this. I hope my wife or my kids don't come walking around. . . ." When it comes on, turn it off. A pre-decision.

When someone starts to flirt or come on to you at the supermarket, at church, or at the stoplight. Someone gives you a little wink or an inappropriate comment, and you can feel the faint tune of the dance start. You may think, "Oh, this makes me feel young again. I must still be attractive!" Or if you're a man, you kind of stick out your chest, suck in your gut, and think, "Yeah, I don't think I can hold this for very long, but—I've still got it!" Long before any involvement ever gets close, make a pre-decision. When someone flirts, you get businesslike and say, "Excuse me, ma'am or sir, would you like to go ahead." And don't make eye contact again.

The same principles apply to certain magazines, stores, and movies. Pre-deciding is not about being legalistic; it's about being honest and realistic about yourself and God's prescription in your life. Pre-deciding is the mark of someone who understands that what goes into your mind will always come out in your life. Many of us play the game of "Love-lite" or "Light-lite," wondering if we can get away with just tiptoeing in love instead of walking in love, or if we can walk on the edge of light instead of right in the middle of God's spotlight. Here's the game we play: "Let's see, here's the line, here's the blatant sin. How close can I get without falling in?" God doesn't put barriers and warning signs up so that we will try to live right next to them. Rather, he gives us these so we'll run the other way!

Don't ask what other Christians are doing to determine what you will do. Judging by our divorce rate and dysfunctional families, too many believers are making the same mistakes the world is making. We say we are living in the Light, but often we are living in darkness. We surveyed the sixth-graders in one church and discovered that 80 percent of them watched R-rated movies regularly. Is it any surprise that some of their older brothers and sisters showed up for counseling because of promiscuity, pregnancies, and sexually transmitted diseases?

As we said, we always reap what we sow. Planting convictions is a major pre-decision. Don't expect corn if you planted squash. But our convictions will be challenged. When we say, "I'm not going to go there, and neither is my family," our kids will say, "That's not fair—all my friends are going there." We have to pre-decide our answer and stick to it. "That's okay. I guess I love you more than their parents love them." That answer worked for Theresa and me in raising four active kids.

Make a pre-decision about how far you will go with the opposite sex when you are dating. Make a pre-decision where you will go on the date and what time you will take your date home. Make a pre-decision about what parties you will go to and when you're going to leave. Make a pre-decision about what you will do when you see certain magazines or movies. Make a pre-decision for how you will respond when someone else's wife or husband starts unloading about problems and dissatisfaction at home, sharing things you don't need to hear. "You know what, it's obvious that you need to talk to a counselor or someone who can really help your situation." Or, "Would you like to talk to my wife?" Yes, it feels rude to cut someone off who seems to be reaching out for help, but we're actually helping them more by getting ourselves out of that situation. Great intentions can easily get sidetracked into terrible mistakes.

Step 4. Get Accountability

Develop convictions, ponder the consequences, make pre-decisions, and then, finally, take the fourth intentional step of getting accountability. Asking others to help you keep your commitments to God will empower you to walk pleasing to the Lord. Identify two or three people who will boldly and regularly check with you about your commitments. The Bible didn't say walk alone as a child of the light; rather, we are to "walk as children of the light." God's prescription for living and loving must be carried out by individuals in community. Every New Testament command that I can find is in the second person plural. In Texas, they say "y'all," and this phrase fits well here. "Y'all walk as children of the light." I can't do this on my own, nor can you. But together we can experience God's power and fellowship.

> Asking others to help you keep your commitments to God will empower you to walk pleasing to the Lord.

For years now I've maintained an accountability group. In fact, the elders, staff, and ministry teams at our church have an accountability component built into them. At a recent meeting we broke into groups of three and asked, "How are you doing in your thought life? How are you doing in your sexual relationship and your purity? What specific steps do you need to take to shore up that area and make it stronger before God?" We shot it straight with one another. We accepted one another. We know and expect that there will be occasional failure and that we will need to help and strengthen each other toward getting back on track and walking in purity.

Do you have someone you can really trust who will ask you questions like those? You must pre-decide to have that kind of relationship or you will fail. But let's remember, no accountability group is fail-safe. We are all easily deceived, and left to ourselves we will lie to one another, even in accountability groups that were organized for openness and honesty. One of the commitments I've made is to tell the truth even when it's uncomfortable or threatens other people's impressions of me. All of us desperately need accountability. Why? In order to fulfill the closing thought in Ephesians 5:8–10, "to learn what is pleasing to the Lord" (NASB). A committed small group of believers can do wonders in each other's life using this process of honest, soul-searching accountability.

God Wants All of You

Let me close this chapter with these thoughts. The apostle Paul in the Ingram Amplified Version says in Romans 12:1, *"Therefore, I urge you, brothers [and sisters], in view of God's mercy"*— here's what I want, I urge you—*"to offer your bodies as living sacrifices."* God doesn't want your religion, he doesn't want your money, and he doesn't want your good works. He wants you—body and all. Everything else flows out of this basic commitment.

What kind of "living sacrifice" is he talking about? One that is *"holy and pleasing to God—this is your spiritual act of worship."* The very best way that we can say yes to genuine love and no to second-rate sex is to come to our Creator and give ourselves wholly back to him. Being a "living sacrifice" is a great oxymoron and the best life a person could experience. It means embarking on a daily adventure in which every decision, action, thought, and intention can be traced back to the desire to live for God sacrificially. It means sacrificing comfortable but sinful habits in order to say yes to love. It means pre-deciding in major areas of life because we already know that left to the last moment, our decisions will be the wrong ones. But it also means being truly alive!

Romans 12:2 goes on with the thought *"Do not conform any longer to the pattern of this world, but be transformed by the renewing of your mind."* Throughout this book we have been challenging a formula and a pattern that rules this world. Our objective is to break that pattern—that mold—and live freely by God's prescription, especially in the relational and sexual aspects of life. We're told here that this process will require our minds to be transformed. How? By the renewing of our minds—by training them to approach life with a different mental framework.

The reason I have personally pre-decided not to watch R-rated movies or view nudity of any kind is not because I'm a prude. I just know that it will put thoughts in my mind that will haunt me and tempt me. If I sow these images in my mind, I will reap results I don't want to reap. So I've developed some specific convictions that are right for me. I've pondered the consequences of failure and made some pre-decisions about what I will think about, watch, and do. And I have a few close friends to help me keep my commitments to God. The results have been not a life of restrictions and frustrations but a life better than I ever dreamed possible. I think often and gratefully about all God has allowed me to share with Theresa over the last twenty-five years with regard to love, sex, and a lasting, secure relationship. I'm reminded of the last part of Romans 12:2, which promises that as we say no to the world's system and yes to God's way, we then will be able to test and *"prove what the will of God is—that which is good, acceptable, and perfect"* (NASB).

Has the struggle for sexual purity been difficult? Yes! Countercultural? Yes! Have I had to make some tough decisions about delayed gratification? You bet! Have I had to make renewing my mind a priority? Of course! But I'm here to tell you that the depth of love and rich relationship you are longing for is only available when you cooperate with the Creator's design.

So how about you? How would describe the present state of your relationships? Is sexual purity a strength in your life or an area of struggle, frustration, and guilt? Are you willing to stop, step back, and reevaluate your attitudes and actions with regard to sexual purity? Would you be willing to prayerfully consider developing some specific convictions for yourself in this arena and then come up with a personal game plan for your life?

The questions below will help you begin the journey. After you have done the private work, I hope you will find a mature, trustworthy friend or pastor and talk about how to implement the game plan God gives you. Why? Because the loving relationship you want demands sexual purity, and sexual purity demands a game plan!

Personal Evaluation

1. When you read the five statistical facts about sex early in this chapter, which ones provided you with the strongest motivation to be sexually pure? Why?

2. In what ways has your personal sexual history in relationships demonstrated the truth of this chapter?

3. To what degree do the lessons and pain in your past cause you to agree that God's way is in your best interest?

4. Which of the four aspects of "God's Game Plan for Sexual Purity" do you need to put into practice this week?

    a. Develop Convictions
    b. Ponder the Consequences
    c. Pre-decide Your Actions
    d. Get Accountability

5. List two or three names of people you have asked or will ask to help you keep your commitments and your game plan.

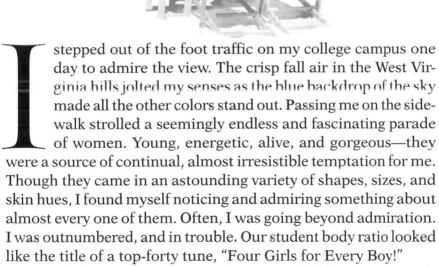

9

The Romance of Purity

I stepped out of the foot traffic on my college campus one day to admire the view. The crisp fall air in the West Virginia hills jolted my senses as the blue backdrop of the sky made all the other colors stand out. Passing me on the sidewalk strolled a seemingly endless and fascinating parade of women. Young, energetic, alive, and gorgeous—they were a source of continual, almost irresistible temptation for me. Though they came in an astounding variety of shapes, sizes, and skin hues, I found myself noticing and admiring something about almost every one of them. Often, I was going beyond admiration. I was outnumbered, and in trouble. Our student body ratio looked like the title of a top-forty tune, "Four Girls for Every Boy!"

Though the memories are over thirty years old, they remain vivid. I don't actually remember the girls' faces and I never knew many of their names, but I clearly recall the internal battle that raged in my heart and mind during those days among so many sights, sounds, and smells of beauty. I had been a Christian less than two years and was just beginning to experience the real struggle between ingrained habits from my background and the new desires that Christ had placed in my heart. When it came to my intention to view women with respect and purity, I found I had a whole new understanding of the implications of the biblical phrase "the spirit is willing but the flesh is weak!" Glances tinged with lust seemed second nature to me. Constant guilt made me desperate for solutions—few of them practical. Part of me just wanted to walk around with my eyes shut tight all the time, while another part of me mocked the idea as pointless because I already had plenty of images recorded to play back on the inside of my eyelids.

I knew that when God forgave my sins, he set me on a new journey. I was certainly traveling with Christ, but I was still carrying a lot of baggage from my past. The lessons I had learned from the world about how to do relationships hadn't been challenged. In fact, my continual failures in relationships and lapses into lust seemed to add more baggage to my load every day. Eventually, I voiced my frustration to God. I demanded, "Why did you give me all these hormones and all these desires, send me to a college where there are four girls for every guy, and then constantly remind me that the ways I want to look and the things I want to do are forbidden? Is this your idea of a joke? Are you a cosmic killjoy?"

Of course, getting angry at God didn't help my guilt load, so I would try to balance the weight by making fresh commitments to maintain purity by sheer willpower. I made tearful promises to God about avoiding sin that I broke before the streaks dried on my face. I really didn't get God's plan. I didn't have the background of biblical insight and life examples to give me hope. I didn't understand God's character, and I wasn't really convinced that he had my best in mind, not just for eternity but also for my daily life. My continual failures simply heaped up feelings of helplessness, stupidity, and discontentment.

Love Lived Out

In spite of all this confusion, God continued to work in my life. During this time of turmoil, I got involved in a little church in town where a grocery store, gas station, post office, a bar, and another equally small church all shared Main Street. The population on our campus outnumbered the town folk by a few thousand, but I enjoyed spending time each week with people at church who were not my age. At that church I met a couple, Dave and Lanny, who had become Christians about the same time I had. I admit I thought they were really old, perhaps early thirties, but having just turned twenty myself, I was impressed by their maturity.

Dave and Lanny launched our relationship by inviting me over for dinner. I got in my little Volkswagen Bug and wandered a winding four or five miles into the hills to find their house. A free, home-cooked meal sounded like a feast to my ears and stomach. I never thought of them as poor, but they lived in a very old farmhouse. The yard was clean but bare, with a few tufts of grass in a yard that had been worn down by two active kids. The house was white clapboard with chipping paint, but the lights in the windows glowed with welcome that evening. Inside, I was greeted with mouthwatering odors and the smiles of kids. As Dave took my coat, I couldn't help but notice the sparse furniture and the missing doors that had been replaced by hanging sheets in several doorways. None of the assorted chairs in the kitchen matched the gaudy table with the sticky top, bizarre flower pattern, and oddly shaped metal round legs. But a simple cloth covered most of the table, and the inexpensive place settings accomplished their primary purpose—holding piles of mashed potatoes, savory gravy, and roast beef long enough for me to satisfy my hunger.

The pictures in my memory of that evening exude extravagance not because of the surroundings but because of the abundance of love that filled that kitchen. I felt encircled, lifted, and then filled with it. It was more satisfying than the delicious meal and yet so simple that I might not have noticed it looking from the outside. Dave, Lanny, and their two children aged five and three made a space for a struggling college student in their family circle that night and gave me a gift I have treasured ever since. The effect was subtle. We just sat and ate, talked, and laughed, as a family. I was absorbed into their wholeness. All my hormonal struggles and trying to do what was right came under a new influence that night. A few times in the course of the meal I noticed the way Dave looked at his wife. Sometimes their fingers touched when they passed bowls to each other. And I caught the smile that Lanny had for him. I could tell that this was more than just a good friendship. They were pretty excited about each other. There was a warmth in that house, and the kids seemed to bask in the glow of their parents' love. Long before dessert arrived, I found myself thinking, "I don't know what the future holds, but someday I want to have what I see happening around this table."

By the time supper was over, droopy eyes and yawns announced bedtime for the kids. Dave turned to me and said, "Excuse us for a few minutes. We're pretty new Christians so we're still figuring some things out, but we have a little routine that we do at night."

"Oh, go ahead. Don't worry about me," I replied.

They disappeared behind a sheet that curtained their children's doorway, and I sat at the table, fascinated by what I heard. Informed by the murmured instructions and soft noises, I could see that little family kneeling beside a bed. Mom helped the little kids fold their hands, and dad shared a little bit about just who Jesus was and how much he cared for them and their new friend, Chip. Then Dave prayed, followed by Lanny, and then I heard the voices of those little kids, talking simply and trustingly to their heavenly Father. Tucking-in noises, giggles, night-night hugs, and kisses followed. Dave and Lanny came back out and we quietly talked and shared coffee and apple pie for a while longer. The evening flew by, but I didn't want to leave.

I vividly remember the drive down the hills back to campus. On that windy, West Virginia back road I had a serious conversation with God. "Lord, that's what I want. More than a high, more than some pleasure, more than manipulating some girl, there's a hunger so deep in me for what they have—that's what I want. I want a relationship like theirs. I want a family like they have. Lord, how can it be?"

And it was as if the Spirit of God spoke to me almost audibly, "Chip, you know those boundaries that you keep chafing against? You know those commands that I have given that you don't understand? You know those concepts about purity? The reason I've given all of those is not because I want to reduce your pleasure. I want to increase your pleasure. I want you to delay gratification not because I don't want you to get the best, but because I want you to get the very best."

As I pulled onto campus, Romans 8:32 popped into my mind as bright as a neon sign: "He who did not spare his own Son, but gave him up for us all—how will he not also, along with him, graciously give us all things?" Even as I said the words out loud I knew that they applied to me in an immediate, life-changing way. I can't describe to you what happened to me that night other than my mind did a 180-degree turn. I realized the purpose behind all the commands of God was the love of God—God was on my team! God gave all those instructions and caused me to feel grieved and guilty when I violated or doubted his directions because he wanted me to have what this little family had. I knew any other approach to relationships would turn out to be second best. Anything else is filled with heartache, destruction, using people, and all kinds of different choices that bring sorrow. That little experience was like getting a clear and unforgettable snapshot of what it means to walk in the light.

> I realized the purpose behind all the commands of God was the love of God—God was on my team!

From that night, my life took a new direction when it came to the issue of sexual purity. Did I still have struggles? Yes. Did I still do some things I was ashamed of? Yes. Did I have some ups and downs? Oh, yes! But instead of picturing God on the other side of the fence issuing harsh orders that took all the fun out of life, I now understood God was on my team, and he was helping me get the very best, because I was his son.

The Bible points out that where there is no vision—where there is no revelation in the sense that there's no truth from God's Word—then the people go unrestrained, out of control, without direction. ***"But blessed [happy] is he [or she] who keeps the*** *law [God's Word]"* (Prov. 29:18). That night I made a decision because I saw the truth in God's Word and because I witnessed God's truth lived out. In my heart I said, "Lord, I'm willing to do it your way because no matter what it takes or how difficult the way becomes for me, what I saw and felt tonight is what I want in my life." God has been absolutely faithful to every part of his lesson in the years that have passed since that night.

The Power of Light

The unfolding love song we have been listening to throughout Ephesians 5 began with a simple overture, a haunting tune about "walking in love." We recognize that tune everywhere in life but wonder if we'll ever be able to sing along. In the initial verses, the melody alternated between heavy sounds of warning and caution (avoid sexual immorality, impurity, greed) and the light, uplifting sounds of Christ's love song, recalling the extent to which he went to express his love as well as the call to imitate him in the way we love. The music picked up in volume and clarity, including lyrics about "walking in light" and trumpeting the character of godly living that exhibits goodness, righteousness, and truth. Now we're ready for the final crescendo of truth.

The final passage we will look at in Ephesians 5 begins with a softer, sadder melody of warning and grief over the conditions of the world and the lengths to which we must go to keep from being dragged back into a way of life we no longer desire. It will lead to a crescendo of truth that will bring us to a decision point. Ephesians 5:11–14 tells us why sex is such serious business to God:

> Do not participate in the unfruitful deeds of darkness, but instead even expose them; for it is disgraceful even to speak of the things which are done by them in secret. But all things become visible when they are exposed by the light, for everything that becomes visible is light. For this reason it says,

"Awake, sleeper,
And arise from the dead,
And Christ will shine on you." [NASB]

The subject matter in these verses clearly relates to sexual behavior. The forceful command forbids us from "participating" in these activities, meaning don't be connected with or associate with this way of life. Notice that the "deeds of darkness" are to be avoided, not people. Jesus hung out with a lot of people involved in sexual immorality, but he didn't participate in it. In fact, his presence accomplished what the next phrase describes—Jesus exposed immorality. The word *expose* has an interesting history. It means "to convict or reprove." It's used throughout the New Testament for bringing something into the light so that the object, attitude, or person can be clearly seen. Why is exposure necessary? The next verse provides the reason—because these secret things are shameful and disgraceful to discuss. God sees sex as such a mysterious and holy thing that even the discussion of sexual perversion among God's people is prohibited.

If you are following this line of reasoning, you can see we have a problem. How are we to expose what is too disgraceful to talk about? How are we going to bring the light of truth to bear on the shameful secrets in people's lives if we are not to speak of these things? Ephesians 5:13 provides the answer.

> We are to expose the world's dysfunctional attitude toward sex, not by what we say, but by how we live.

The idea here is that the way to reprove the world is not by getting together to talk about all the perverted aspects of sex outside of marriage. Those discussions easily become verbal voyeurism. He says don't go there. Don't expose immorality by talk; *expose it with light*. That's the message of verse 13. The powerful imagery of light carries throughout these verses. Those who "walk in the light" will expose the deeds done in darkness by the light of their lives. We are to expose the world's dysfunctional attitude toward sex, not by what we say, but by how we live. Talking in this setting is like cursing the darkness, when we would be much farther ahead to light a candle.

Light brings amazing transforming power to bear in any situation. Jesus had an intentional purpose in mind when he told us we were the light of the world (Matt. 5:14–16). Light isn't loud; it's silent. Jesus didn't tell us to outshout the world but to shed his light. In the darkness our voices get lost among other voices. But darkness cowers before light. There are certain kinds of bacteria that multiply explosively in the darkness, but the moment you bring them into the sunlight, they die instantly. They can't handle exposure. What is true in the physical world is also true in the spiritual world. John 3:19–21 describes the effect Jesus had on the world: *"This is the verdict: Light has come into the world, but men loved darkness instead of light because their deeds were evil. Everyone who does evil hates the light, and will not come into the light for fear that his deeds will be exposed. But whoever lives by the truth comes into the light, so that it may be seen plainly that what he has done has been done through God."*

God's Wake-Up Call

As we approach the final sections of this book, I am acutely aware that the average reader will not necessarily be someone who feels accomplished and confident in the art of relationships. I know those who are weighed down will greatly outnumber those starting out, hopeful of doing it God's way from the beginning. You may have felt a surge of hopelessness even as you read my story because it seems too late for you. Each time I have mentioned the subject of hope in these pages, I have done so hearing the questions of so many who fearfully ask, "After all I've done, can God really do something with my life? After all my unintentional mistakes and even my willful, stubborn choices to go against God, can I still experience his mercy and healing? What can God do with a life filled with so much that can't seem to be undone?"

My answer to all these questions is the same. God's grace, applied through Jesus Christ, is greater than you can imagine. As you read these words today, what really matters isn't what you've already done but what you will do next. It's time for you to hear God's wake-up call.

Wake up! When it comes to love, sex, and lasting relationships, our culture has been asleep at the wheel for years. Even Christians have nodded off when they should have been paying attention. Wake up! There's a better way to do relationships—God's way! The verses in Scripture we have looked at repeatedly in this book include a crescendo of truth for those who want to experience all that God has planned for them.

As we have already discovered, throughout Scripture we find that sexuality and worship intersect. God has given you and me a passion button in our hearts. The God who deeply enjoys the act of creating and made us in his image gave us a parallel sense of pleasure in the act of creation. There's divine mystery in sexuality. This explains why almost every false religion involves some sort of sexual expression. This also explains why I've never met a man or a woman who has a victorious, close relationship with God who hasn't dealt with the sexual issues in their lives. Because until you become pure, until you think, speak, and live out God's commands in the sexual arena, you will always consciously or unconsciously be involved in false worship. Your worship will be for your desires and lust, and it will involve using people to accomplish the purpose of your worship, which is to satisfy yourself. Jesus flatly declared no one can serve two masters (Matt. 6:24). If we are not consciously serving God, we are serving ourselves in some way. It's time to declare whom we will worship with our lives as well as with our lips.

Love, Sex, and the Gospel

That night so long ago in West Virginia, I was visiting a friendly family, but in truth I walked into the light. The light of Dave and Lanny and the living products of that love—two lovely children—exposed my life. Under their roof I basked in the glow of sexual purity and loving, lasting relationships. That light exposed my perverted view of sex and my twisted view of relationships. There was no room to hide, and I didn't want to. Dave and Lanny didn't probe my past or level charges about "the way college students behave." Yet in the light of what God had given them, I saw myself for who I was in the area of purity.

The light not only forced me to make a choice (to remain in darkness or walk in the light), it also seemed to flow into me, giving me the strength to say, "I'm going to live my life God's way." I began to learn that night why sex is such serious business to God. Sex and the relationship he designed to protect and nourish it turns out to be one of the strongest evangelistic tools Christians have. Love, sex, and a lasting relationship done God's way presents an irrefutable argument for the gospel of Jesus Christ.

In fact, notice the last lines in the verses from Ephesians we quoted above: ***"For this reason it says, 'Awake, sleeper, / And arise from the dead, / And Christ will shine on you.'"*** When the unbelieving world sees us living out sexually pure lives and deep, loving, authentic relationships, they will be brought to the same decision I faced on my way home from Dave and Lanny's. The light that shines when God's prescription for living flows through our lives will help people see their sexual mores "in a whole new light" and show them their need for Christ.

The verse tells us to wake up and get up. There's a world that's sleepwalking through life, following a nightmare rather than the truth. They are trying to do relationships. They want to be loved. They long to be connected. They've got hormones, they don't know how it works, so they try the formula that gets whispered in their ears. They see it acted out on the silver screen by people whose real lives demonstrate they can't live the way their characters live. Sleepwalking people discover the Hollywood formula doesn't work with one person, so they try another person, then another, just one step from despair.

Some of the sleepwalkers give up on real people and instead immerse themselves in the gloom of pornography or sit in front of computer screens and carry on multiple cyber-relationships complete with pseudointimacy. They fill their heads with images that eventually distort reality even more. Think of it this way. How many devices can you name that each of us has readily available whose primary purpose is to keep a typical person sleepwalking through life, eyes tightly shut against the light of truth? Could it be that most of what we call entertainment is actually a sedative that keeps us from awakening to the light?

The biggest problem with sleepwalking through life is that it isn't really living. Eventually it results in chaos: despair, destruction, pain, sexual disease, broken homes, and relational wreckage. Jesus told us that he came so that we could have life—the real thing! (See John 10:10.) Into this world of darkness God calls us to live in a winsome, loving way so that Christ will shine on those who wake up and give them abundant life. **Just as light silently reveals all things for what they really are, so it is when God's people "model" purity and love in relationships. They expose sexual immorality for what it really is: lustful, destructive self-worship.**

The Reward for Sexual Purity Is Awesome!

At this point, you may find yourself reeling inside. Stuck in the middle of a terrible situation, overwhelmed by past failures or full of doubts, perhaps you are thinking, "I can't even begin to imagine that my life could be a light to someone else. I know what darkness is like. But how can I reflect God's light to others when I myself am still spending too much time sleepwalking?"

Let me assure you that God understands all that you are going through and he wants to help you. The price tag of sexual purity may seem high, but the rewards are great.

You may have thought several times as you've read these chapters, "Chip, your news is a little too late for me. You don't know my background. I've looked for intimacy in all the wrong ways. I've looked to belong in all the wrong places. I've been in a number of relationships—nothing's left but emotional scars."

You're right—I don't know your story, but God does. He knows every intimate, shameful, and sorrowful detail. And his love for you has never wavered for a moment. It's never too late. You can draw a line in the sand today and say, "By the grace of God, I'm going to come to Jesus. I'm going to tell him I'm sorry for my past. I'm going to ask him to forgive me. I'm going to make a personal commitment that in my mind, in my speech, in my life, from here on by his power and strength, I'm going to be pure. Based on Christ's grace and forgiveness, I'm going to consider myself a 'reborn virgin,' mentally, spiritually, and even physically. I'm going to start walking in love and strolling in the light!" Does that sound wild? It is. It's even miraculous. That's the romance of purity, and God wants to share it with you.

Will there be some consequences to deal with? Sure. Some baggage to get rid of, with God's help? Of course. You can't imagine just how deep and wonderful the grace of God is, but you can start getting a better idea by trusting him. He'll forgive. He'll cleanse and restore you. Neither Theresa nor I grew up in Christian homes. What I have shared with you in this book was completely foreign to us even after coming to personal faith in Christ. Fortunately, early in our spiritual journey, God brought wise mentors into our lives to help us deal with past guilt, unload garbage, and learn God's prescription for doing relationships.

By the time Theresa and I met, each of us had purposed in our hearts to abandon Hollywood's formula and to build our relationship following God's design and prescription.

We began by learning to communicate openly and honestly as friends. We made the spiritual aspects of our relationship the first priority. We worked out a simple game plan for our relationship and kept each other accountable for our actions. We held the romantic and physical aspects of our relationship "in check"—moving ahead wisely and slowly according to God's leading. We learned about one another's heart for God by observing each other in nonromantic settings that allowed and required us to be ourselves rather than "do the dance" and play the game.

Did we have struggles and difficult times? Yes. Did we have to work through past baggage and learn a whole new way of relating without many examples to guide us? Certainly. Did we do it perfectly? No. But looking back, I see how even two people with full "pasts" to overcome were led by God to develop their relationship in a revolutionary manner. Following God's prescription has resulted in the kind of love, sex, and lasting (almost twenty-five-year) relationship that neither of us dreamed possible. My point is simple. God can and will do for you, no matter how much baggage you may have, what he's done for us.

A Word to Virgins

Lest we assume or give the impression that "everybody's doing it," I have an important word of encouragement for those who are virgins. Following a presentation of these ideas that I made recently, a handsome thirty-three-year-old guy came up to talk to me. He looked around to make sure we were out of earshot and in a whisper confessed, "Hey, I'm a virgin. But it feels kind of weird in our day to be a virgin."

I didn't know whether to cry or cheer. I said, "You know what? You're not weird—you're wise. And you're not alone either. Hang in there; it will be worth it." Isn't it amazing how often people who are engaged in sexual perversions are cheered and supported when they "come out of the closet"? Meanwhile, when virgins reveal their stance, they get maligned and treated as strange and abnormal.

If I could tell you how to avoid sexually transmitted diseases; how to give your marriage a 50 percent better chance of surviving; and how to live a guiltless, healthy, satisfying life, would you be interested? Almost everyone in our culture would say, "Sure, tell me how?" They would be shocked and perhaps dismayed with the answer. It begins with sexual purity—virginity. Those who still have it also have an excellent opportunity to miss out on most of the painful baggage that comes with the Hollywood formula. Being a virgin isn't weird; it's profoundly wise.

> Being a virgin isn't weird; it's profoundly wise.

Wake Up for the Revolution

Having served in a local church for many years, I have taken part in numerous wedding services and had extensive conversations with many couples preparing for marriage. From this experience I've seen that there are light-years of difference between those who do engagement and marriage the world's way and those who do it God's way. I can also tell you that by the time a couple meets with their pastor, they usually have made the choice of which way they are going to go. Premarital counseling is very worthwhile but often much of its value is nullified by the choices a couple has already made before counseling begins.

It's an interesting historical note that the premarital counseling movement really got started in the late 1960s as a reaction to the "sexual revolution." But premarital counseling cannot undo in six to eight sessions what a couple has ingested from the culture in twenty years. What we need is a countercultural movement among Christians to let God's light shine. We need a spiritual revolution quietly led by believers who decide we're going to place our own marriages and families under the light and start getting rid of the darkness. If, as the Bible says, judgment begins in the household of God (see 1 Peter 4:17), then let's allow the purifying effects of God's prescription to make a sweeping, revolutionary change in our lives as believers. The world will notice the difference. They may laugh at first, but many of the sleepwalkers will wake up and be drawn into the light as they see authentic love, depth, and passion playing out in our lives.

In the final chapter, I invite you to join me in answering God's call to a **second sexual revolution**. There is a revolutionary way to build relationships with the opposite sex—a way that produces intimacy, not guilt, a way built on love, not lust, a way that results in satisfying sex and long-term commitment.

Personal Evaluation

1. Dave and Lanny made a lasting impression on my life and set a shining example of what a marriage could be. Who are your best examples of healthy relationships and marriage? Why?

2. After reading this chapter, how would you now explain why sex is such serious business with God?

3. How have you experienced the truth of the statement "You don't expose immorality by talk; you expose it with light"?

4. Why is there such a cultural aversion to virginity in our times?

5. On a scale of one to ten, how would you rank your own sexual purity in mind, word, and deed? Write a sentence or two to explain your answer.

Answering God's Wake-Up Call to the "Second Sexual Revolution"

God's prescription for love, sex, and lasting relationships turns out to be powerful medicine. Like today's cancer-fighting drugs, God's prescription may feel as if it's killing you on the way to giving you life. It will create immediate and painful confrontations in your life with the status quo. Effective medicine is like that. But we've been convinced by the world that God's prescription won't taste good or do any good. Instead, we've become used to taking the sickening sweet potion offered by the world and have refused to recognize the deadly side effects it brings.

The Hollywood formula turns out to be poison. I hope by now you realize that not only are God's commands concerning sexual purity for our personal good, they also challenge the cancer of ignorance, immorality, and faithlessness that has infected our culture.

183

A Call to Revolution

The world needs nothing short of a revolution. Our lives, homes, and churches need to become cells of people who walk in love and live in light. We don't need to rant and rave about the way things are; we need to take regular, consistent doses of God's prescription. The world will not be convinced by shouting; the world will be convinced by light. We don't need to pump up the volume; we need to turn on the lights!

How will we do that? How can we really make a difference against an opponent that seems to have already won the hearts and minds of people all around us? How do we mount a revolution to take back the soul of our culture? **We answer God's call to a second sexual revolution.** I mean that literally, not just as a motivational slogan or hyperbole. I invite you to join me and tens of thousands of other Christians all over America who believe that our culture is ready for a second revolution concerning sex.

Think back for a moment (if you're old enough) to the 1960s and recall how the first so-called sexual revolution was ignited. A small countercultural group of people called into question the status quo. They openly challenged the current thinking about sexual fidelity and preached "free love" and peace as the alternative lifestyle. They modeled their message with their lives and proclaimed it through their music and art. They proudly wore the label of radicals, taking on every form of authority—summed up in "the Establishment." They mixed the natural uncertainties and curiosities of youth with a strong dose of rebelliousness and created a philosophy of life. The results have been shocking. In one short generation (forty years), an entire culture's morals, values, and practices have changed.

So where's the hope? What changed in one direction can be reversed. The steps we took deeper into the darkness can be retraced toward the light if people like you and I are willing to be just as radical for the truth as those in the 1960s were for a lie. Those youthful rebels were sincerely sold out to an illusion, but it drove them to transform a culture. You may have been among them and realize now that it wasn't wrong to be absolutely committed—the problems came from being absolutely committed to the wrong ideals. Just imagine how exciting it would be to live with that same kind of abandon, only now for the truth. What would happen if the first decade of the new millennium was remembered as the time when "Walk in love and walk in light" became as culture-changing as "Make love, not war"? How would the world respond to Christians who actually lived what they preach? Wouldn't you want to be among those who made a difference for right? We can!

How to Launch a Revolution

The rebellion against the world's system has to begin with our thinking. A big part of the problem can be traced back to our acceptance of a dichotomy between God's ways and the world's ways. As believers, we have been duped and brainwashed into thinking that we can think about everything except sex from God's point of view. We think that God is either disinterested or uncomfortable with sex. Those assumptions represent the thinking of darkness. God thought sex was a great idea; that's why he created it! The world has all kinds of problems with sex because it has problems with God.

> The rebellion against the world's system has to begin with our thinking.

But our minds are only one of the battlegrounds in this revolution. In fact, the second sexual revolution we're talking about must advance simultaneously on three fronts. We must develop:

1. A new way to think about sexuality
2. A new way to attract the opposite sex
3. A new way to relate to the opposite sex

If we can accomplish these three missions, at the very minimum our personal lives will be radically transformed. At the maximum we will have participated in the transformation of a culture. In the next few pages we will explore what each of these fronts will demand of us.

A Second Sexual Revolution Demands a New Way to Think about Sexuality

When we think in a revolutionary and godly way about sex, our minds will be filled with three radical thoughts. These are the basics of the revolution. You and I won't overthrow an entrenched system without a focused, persistent, nonnegotiable alternative that absolutely flies in the face of almost everything we see and hear in our culture. The revolution begins with these three radical claims: (1) sex is sacred, (2) sex is serious, and (3) sex is a grave responsibility.

Radical Claim 1—Sex Is Sacred

Until you and I recognize that sex is sacred to God, we haven't joined the revolution. Do you want to stand with God? Then sex is sacred. Do you want to find a battle line in our culture? Try saying "sex is sacred" in conversation. Deliberately use the phrase when someone asks you why you don't watch certain movies or other "entertainment." You will be challenged. You will have rebelled against the establishment. Claiming that sex is sacred is like burning the flag of the Hollywood formula. Be prepared for reactions. Be ready to explain exactly what you mean when you say sex is sacred. You may feel a little lonely, but don't forget, every time you say "Sex is sacred," God responds with "I agree."

The sacredness of sex means sex is holy. It's set apart as a meaningful and powerful gift that reminds us constantly of God. Sex is a special, intimate grant from God. Hebrews 13:4 states, ***"Marriage should be honored by all, and the marriage bed kept pure, for God will judge the adulterer and all the sexually immoral."*** The truth about sexuality doesn't get any clearer than this beautiful picture and stern warning. Sex—the marriage bed—should be honored and kept pure. The relationship called marriage is to be set apart and kept undefiled. Sex is sacred because it offers us a unique opportunity to be grateful to God with one other person.

Imagine thinking about sex that way. This kind of mindset would mean that sex is never treated as common or casual. It's treated with special respect. It resembles in some ways the crystal and china we keep at home for special occasions. We value these items because they are holy in the sense that they are set apart for special use. The sacredness of valuable possession pales before the sacredness of sex. That's how God wants us to think about sex. At its most intimate, sex is about *knowing*, not lying or sleeping together. When Adam and Eve began to explore their sexuality, the Bible describes their intercourse by saying "Adam knew Eve." The moment was sacred, holy. Each one of them in God's design was opening up the holy of holies of their life, coming together spiritually, physically, emotionally.

Much later in the Bible, when King David sinned by committing adultery with Bathsheba, a different word was used for the same physical act, "David . . . lay with her" (see 2 Sam. 11:1–5 NASB). Although David knew Bathsheba was another man's wife, he lusted after her as a sexual object and took her as a plaything. The consequences were horrendous—a seed of immorality was planted in his household that yielded a harvest of destroyed lives.

Sex isn't just about body parts fitting together or momentary pleasure—it's about heart and personhood. It's about mystery. It's about sacredness. Sex was never meant to sell stuff. Sex was never meant to be a way to get a cheap laugh. Sex was never something to be viewed casually as if for entertainment. It is to be a sacred, holy thing.

When you start treating sex as holy and saying that sex is sacred, you will be living a radical life. That radical claim will echo through your life like the shot heard 'round the world that launched a different revolution long ago. You will have opened up the first front of the second sexual revolution in your life. Are you ready for that kind of commitment?

Radical Claim 2—Sex Is Serious

Do you want to walk in the light and be counted among the rebels in the second sexual revolution? **You will have to make the radical countercultural claim that sex is serious.** Do you want to stand with God? Then sex is serious. Do you long to be treated seriously by those around you? Well, you may not be if you claim that sex is serious, but then again whom are you trying to please? And believe me, as you find other fellow rebels, you will discover some great companions in the revolution.

The Bible sheds blinding light on the seriousness of sexuality in places like 1 Corinthians 6:15–20:

> Do you not know that your bodies are members of Christ himself? Shall I then take the members of Christ and unite them with a prostitute? Never! Do you not know that he who unites himself with a prostitute is one with her in body? For it is said, "The two will become one flesh." But he who unites himself with the Lord is one with him in spirit.
>
> Flee from sexual immorality. All other sins a man commits are outside his body, but he who sins sexually sins against his own body. Do you not know that your body is a temple of the Holy Spirit, who is in you, whom you have received from God? You are not your own; you were bought at a price. Therefore honor God with your body.

The verses above don't give us any room to treat sex lightly. When two people have sex, whether they're married or not, even if it's a fling, or just for pleasure, or if it's with a prostitute, the Scripture says they literally become one flesh. That's how powerful and serious sex is. Do you see the contrast in these verses? We can be united with God following his prescription for relationships or we can be united with a prostitute or be involved in some other second-rate distortion of sexuality. As we have discovered already, sexuality and spirituality always revolve around this issue of worship. When people meet each other in sexual intercourse, a bond of the flesh occurs whether the participants acknowledge it or not. That's how serious sex is. It's not hooking up. It's not casual pleasure. It's not just a little self-satisfaction. The sexual act is a life-uniting act. It's not a game; it's a life-altering decision. That's how serious sex is.

The God of the universe created human beings in such a way that when a man and a woman come together in the confines of marriage, it brings holy pleasure to God. This kind of holy intercourse reflects his desire to bring life! That's why it is the means by which new life is created. The pleasure and potential procreation that reside in sex between those created in God's image makes it worth honoring and protecting. Sex is not to be treated lightly because it is an expression of our deepest human commitment. There should be mystery and holiness and awe.

Don't be surprised when the conflict intensifies as you begin to stand for this claim that sex is serious. Part of the world will tolerate your "religious" statements about sex being sacred. But expect a firestorm of reaction when you claim sex is serious. Are you ready for that kind of revolutionary thinking? Radical results will require radical thinking and living.

Radical Claim 3—Sex Is a Grave Responsibility

Until you and I can think radically beyond ourselves, we won't be part of the second sexual revolution. In a world that has all but forgotten the meaning of the word *responsibility,* God insists that sex is a grave responsibility. Others may decide that claiming sex is sacred and serious are your "private and personal beliefs," but claiming that sex is a grave responsibility will sound to them like an intrusion. You will be accused of trying to make others feel guilty. Remember, radical thinking will affect the way we see and treat others. If you and I want to stand with God, we will make the claim that sex is a grave responsibility. First Thessalonians 4:3–7 says,

> It is God's will that you should be sanctified: that you should avoid sexual immorality; that each of you should learn to control his own body in a way that is holy and honorable, not in passionate lust like the heathen, who do not know God; and that in this matter

no one should wrong his brother or take advantage of him. The
Lord will punish men for all such sins, as we have already told
you and warned you. For God did not call us to be impure, but to
live a holy life.

Where the verses say, "no one should wrong his brother or take
advantage of him," other translations use the term "defraud,"
which captures the idea of arousing sexual desires in another
person that can't be fulfilled legitimately outside of marriage.
We are responsible for the way we present ourselves to others.
If we know someone's weakness and take advantage of it, we
are defrauding him or her. If a woman dresses seductively or a
man manipulates by pretending to care, each is guilty of taking
advantage of someone's vulnerability. The Bible is crystal clear:
Sex outside of the protected enclosure of one man and one woman
in marriage is second-rate, cheap, and destructive.

So why, particularly among Christians, does there seem to be
such a lax attitude and willful ignorance about God's prescription for love, sex, and lasting relationships? Clearly, there has
been a breakdown. The church that claims to follow Jesus often
does not act like it believes that sex is sacred, serious, or a grave
responsibility. Jesus made a number of statements that we have
either forgotten or don't think are important. For example, the
Lord was interacting with some religious leaders when he leveled
the following warning: ***"But if anyone causes one of these little
ones who believe in me to sin, it would be better for him to have
a large millstone hung around his neck and to be drowned in
the depths of the sea"*** (Matt. 18:6). He was talking about spiritual "children," young believers whose hearts are open, people
who want to follow him, people who have seen the light. He was
cautioning those who knew better to be careful, lest they cause
these new believers to stumble.

Jesus continued to speak about the dangers of temptation,
making his warning even more pointed: "How terrible it will be
for anyone who causes others to sin. Temptation to do wrong is
inevitable, but how terrible it will be for the person who does
the tempting" (Matt. 18:7 NLT). Jesus didn't hesitate to hold

people responsible for their input into other people's lives. Do you realize how often in our attitudes in what we laugh at, what we watch, what we pay money for, and how we dress as believers in Jesus Christ that we participate in causing other believers to stumble? We do this so much that it's not even seen as a problem. This is not careless flaunting of freedom in Christ, like the Corinthians did when they ate meat offered to idols (1 Corinthians 8). No, this is an ignorant confusion that sees no contradiction in a message of faith in Christ spoken from the lips while a message of worldly values and immorality is conveyed by our behavior and dress. Both words and actions have meaning, but when they clearly contradict each other, what we actually do matters more.

A radical approach to sexual responsibility asks very different questions when it comes to what we wear, how we look, and how we act. I'm afraid that too often we Christians have used the excuse of freedom in Christ to dress and behave just like the world. That's like claiming freedom while living in bondage. Grave responsibility means we're responsible *to* someone. It means we have to answer to someone for our lives. The radical Christian moves right past questions of style and endless legalistic lists about what believers can't wear or how long they can grow their hair to the core issue: Am I pleasing God? Are the things I'm doing, wearing, and saying pleasing to God? Is there any part of my life that does not honor God? Am I prepared to give a shameless account to my heavenly Father for how I've used this body he gave me?

> I'm afraid that too often we Christians have used the excuse of freedom in Christ to dress and behave just like the world.

We don't expect unbelievers to ask the questions above. We aren't surprised when they reject our radical claims that sex is sacred, serious, and a grave responsibility. But among Christians, the failure to be accountable to each other and to God for the way we live undermines the revolutionary message we have been given to share with the world. I've noticed this particularly in those who have the ear of our young people. Believers who become popular singers or actors carry a clear responsibility to consider the message of what they say or sing and what they do.

There are more and more signs of selling out when it comes to God's standards of sexuality. Visit a Christian bookstore and glance at the covers of albums by Christian recording artists. You will note a trend toward sexual overtones in the photographs. Clothing and poses that project a subtle seductive appeal have been chosen to "attract the market." As radical believers, we're not going to throw stones at these people or call them bad names. We're simply going to say, "This is not how we're going to live. As for me and my house, we're going to serve the Lord."

Sex remains serious in God's eyes, even when God's people treat it as insignificant. Sex was not designed to sell albums or any other product. If we are going to have a sexual revolution among God's people, it will have to start with our minds. We will not be satisfied until we demand of ourselves a revolutionary way of thinking. Now I am not arguing for a return to puritanical attitudes or Victorian customs such as high collars and chastity belts. I am saying that we the church have fallen headfirst into the quagmire of our culture because we don't think rightly about sex. But a renewal in our thought processes will not be enough. We will have to boycott Hollywood's formula for attracting others and incorporate a revolutionary way to develop relationships with the opposite sex.

A Second Sexual Revolution Demands a New Way to Attract the Opposite Sex

One of our first discoveries at the beginning of this book was the point that the Hollywood formula is almost completely based on physical and emotional attraction. This ingrained cultural belief that love grows out of looks must be radically challenged. The second front of the second sexual revolution will directly challenge the way we begin relationships.

The system based on physical and emotional attraction can be found everywhere. You wear clothes that are very tight, pour yourself into your pants, and you can get a lot of attention from the opposite sex. Christian young people, in the wasteland of silence and discomfort about sex in the church, are left to take their cues from the culture. The recent research demonstrates the results we enumerated at the beginning of this book. Some of the effects of the worship of appearance are becoming too obvious to overlook. Now for the first time we see escalating eating disorders among teenage boys. Young men are pumping iron like crazy, taking steroids, and drinking high-protein drinks because they are convinced they have to look a certain way. They're into sex appeal as the best way to attract the opposite sex. For the first time in my life, I'm seeing women come and talk to our counseling staff about their addiction to pornography.

If the world says the way to attract the opposite sex is sex appeal, then seductive dress and a focus on bodies, breasts, and biceps is basically what it boils down to. Manipulation, games, and pseudo-romance are all part of the world's enticing lure. And tragically, we in the church have bought it hook, line, and sinker. Suddenly, the same tragic stories we hear in the world are told in church. We become confused when our kids get involved in destructive relationships; we are confused about why Christians are getting divorced. We live by the world's formula and then wonder why we get the world's results.

Amazingly, God gives three compelling alternatives to mere physical attraction as the basis upon which we can establish relationships with others. Putting these alternatives into action will open up the second front in the second sexual revolution. God's ways to attract the opposite sex may sound at first very old fashioned, but they are very effective. In fact, they are radical. First Peter 3:3–4 says, **"Your beauty should not come from outward adornment, such as braided hair and the wearing of gold jewelry and fine clothes. Instead, it should be that of your inner self, the unfading beauty of a gentle and quiet spirit, which is of great worth in God's sight."**

Radical Way of Attraction #1—Develop Inward Character

You will see the radical nature of God's approach because it offers inward character as an alternative to mere external beauty. This, of course, brings us back to the first step in God's prescription—the issue isn't about finding the right person, it's about being the right person. It's being a godly person—not a prude, not a holier-than-thou stereotype, but a dynamic Christ follower. The radical thinking we discussed in the last section will definitely alter your inward character, and that will be more attractive in the long run than anything you could do to yourself externally.

Radical Way of Attraction #2—Develop Outward Modesty

I think the Lord must have an awesome sense of humor, because he's shaking America's values in unexpected ways. He's using a religious doctor of physiology turned counselor named Dr. Laura. She's got the guts to stand up and declare over the radio waves, "Hey, this is right; this is wrong!" I don't necessarily agree with everything she says, but in a world of relative truth we have a Jewish counselor offering moral answers to millions of people who don't know what to do. She has suffered from backlash that is usually reserved for biblical Christians who dare to speak up.

Another example of God's sense of humor hides behind the startling popularity of a book by twenty-something liberal arts Jewish student Wendy Shalit. She titled it *A Return to Modesty*. In that book she catalogues the fallout among a generation of young adults who have exchanged sex as easily as their parents shook hands. Sex on campus, Shalit explains, is often about as personal as two airplanes refueling. In fact, the custom is called "hooking up." She makes a bright, youthful, and exuberant plea for the need to remember. She challenges our culture to mourn something beautiful that's being lost between the sexes—the loss of modesty.

As we already pointed out, the radical changes in the fabric of experience that have made virginity, privacy, and reserve into something odd or shameful point, not to progress or freedom, but to ugliness. Our loss of basic public decency is something that God must grieve. Something every generation has shared until now is so absent that those growing up in the vacuum feel the loss. The moral threads of our culture have become so frayed that Shalit calls the condition "an invisible American tragedy."[1] Through Shalit's eloquent confessions her generation finds a voice. She shares honestly about the often hidden envy women in her generation feel toward older women who have long-running marriages. She admits to the longings so many of her peers have for lasting relationships and kept commitments. She hopes that many her age will hold out for stability and genuine love instead of settling for the dishonest cheap sexuality and personal degradation that has been, in many ways, forced on the children of our culture.

Wendy has the audacity to call young women of this next millennium to return to modesty in their dress, modesty in their behavior, and to the mystery of sexuality, where some things are kept special, private, and meaningful. She bemoans a culture in which people are so crudely open that there's nothing left to guess or be intrigued about—nothing left to focus on but externals.

I find Wendy Shalit's book refreshing and amazing, especially for one so young. It saddens me, however, that her excellent work and biblical concepts appear to be rarely practiced among the Christian subculture, which intellectually espouses the virtue of modesty. I often wonder what in the world our Christian fathers are thinking when they let their daughters leave the house dressed in ways they know will arouse young men. Yes, I know that there are Christian young people taking a stand, but I daresay that we, the church as a whole, are not backing them up.

Outward modesty has much to do with walking in love and walking in light. All of the shining character qualities that we described when we talked about those two phrases create a delightful and attractive modesty. When we meet someone who holds something in reserve for the person whom he or she will marry, we sense we've met someone with real integrity and personal substance.

Radical Way of Attraction #3—Develop Upward Devotion

The third radical quality the Bible describes can be summarized as upward devotion. How refreshing it is to meet someone who already lives out what we earlier described as the third part of God's formula for love, sex, and lasting relationships—"fixing their hope on God and seeking to please him with their lives." Such a person is living a revolutionary life!

I realize that you may be someone who can honestly say you have never seen what that looks like. Let me tell you, when you see genuine upward devotion in the life of another person, the results are very attractive. In fact, though my wife happens to be outwardly beautiful (especially in my eyes), that was not what attracted me most to her. Theresa's upward devotion was a trait that drew me more powerfully than any outward attraction could have.

I still remember the first time I asked her for a date and she responded that she couldn't go because she had a previous commitment. In the arrogance of my youth I wondered how she could have any previous commitment more important than the chance to spend time with me. Being the snoopy young man that I was, I happened to drive by her house that night, curious about potential competition. Her car was in the driveway, and the lights were on in the living room—she was obviously at home. I reacted with some anger followed quickly by the pang of rejection. I thought she was an amazing woman who was actually interested in me. But how could she choose to spend an evening alone at home rather than being with me?

Two days later my wrong assumptions were corrected by one of her friends. She told me Theresa had shared with her how difficult it had been to turn me down but that she had already set the evening aside to spend time alone with the Lord. The rejection I had felt turned instantly to attraction. How could I not want to be with someone who was committed to her relationship to the Lord in the same way I longed to be? As a result of a very difficult time in her life, Theresa had developed the habit of spending several hours during a couple of evenings per week in prayer and personal communion with God—reading the Bible, singing, and enjoying his presence as her tender heavenly Father. When I realized that I was stood up because God was more important in her life, something clicked inside that I couldn't quite explain. Somehow, being second to God was both a relief and a great attraction. As much as we want people to desire us, an even more powerful and attractive effect enters the relationship when the other person desires God first. By this time in my life I had dated a number of pretty girls and was looking for "the right one." Theresa's upward devotion caused my emotional gears to shift into overdrive, suddenly intent on developing a relationship with a girl who really modeled Christ as first priority in her life.

You see, if you want to build a lasting relationship, it takes more than a nice hairdo, a buffed body, and a good tan. Those things fade quickly and are rather superficial. But when you meet a person with upward devotion, you realize they have substance, character, and a beauty that won't perish with time.

An I.O.U. for the Second Sexual Revolution

As you think about attracting the opposite sex as part of the second sexual revolution, remember that you carry an **I.O.U.**

Inward character
Outward modesty
Upward devotion

Historically, an I.O.U. has been a shorthand way to refer to a debt. The debt that we need to pay in light of all that God has done for us is to do relationships his way. We will do this to promote not only our own good but also his agenda as we walk in the light.

This I.O.U. will involve radical, God-honoring tactics. You may need to throw away some clothes, evaluate your outward appearance, and analyze some of your habits. But remember this: Externals should be a clear and compelling reflection of internals—a deep desire to please God. I don't believe this is a style issue as much as a heart issue. Regardless of your generation's or your own personal taste in clothes, the core issue for those in the second sexual revolution will be: *What am I seeking to communicate by how I dress or how I look?* Ultimately, you need to be able to explain how your external actions and even dress are an expression of your upward devotion to God.

When you and I look in the mirror, we need to think about Colossians 3:17, "And whatever you do, whether in word or deed, do it all in the name of the Lord Jesus, giving thanks to God the Father through him." Every part of our lives can ex-press our debt of gratitude to God as we seek to develop an inward character, outward modesty, and upward devotion that represent we belong to the One who gave his life for us. We don't owe our culture, our peers, or even ourselves anything like the debt of gratitude and love that we owe to the Lord Jesus Christ. You may need help in figuring the specifics of that out for you. **Imagine what would happen if you sat down with three or four close friends whose walk with God you deeply respect and discussed what you wear and why.** What if you actually talked about how low cut is too low, how short or tight will you wear your clothes, and why? What if a few guys openly questioned one another's motives for pumping iron or driving around with sleeveless muscle shirts, and kept each other accountable for healthy living? It's not about what others think or about being conservative or even about pleasing important adults; it's about daring to live radically because you and I desire to please God and do relationships his way.

This I.O.U. will mean that if you are a single person living on the wild side, you will ask, "What messages am I sending?" Here's a shocking bulletin: When you dress or act seductively, you will

> We don't owe our culture, our peers, or even ourselves anything like the debt of gratitude and love that we owe to the Lord Jesus Christ.

attract someone who is exactly like the person you are being. The signals you send will trigger a certain response. So don't be surprised if they don't keep their commitments. Don't be surprised if the next seductive little apple they want to pull off the tree is someone other than you. **This is a fundamental relational principle: You will attract the same kind of person you project or advertise to be.**

The world's strategy is to advertise externally and extravagantly. When a woman puts a sweater on and murmurs, "I wonder how that looks through the eyes of a man?" or when a man sticks on a tight shirt after he's been pumping iron and asks himself, "Will the ladies notice what I've been doing?" these are signs of the Hollywood formula in action. But are there other messages in behaviors like these? Are there some insecurities about our worth that you and I are covering up by advertising externally? Am I trying to project a false image that will attract others based on external signals, or am I committed to an internal integrity that doesn't rely on dishonest external factors?

Are we saying that looking good, pumping iron, and taking care of our bodies is wrong? Absolutely not! I believe that physical fitness contributes to my sense of stewardship of all that God has given to me. I work out regularly and look the best I can. I don't have a problem with people looking good or even good-looking people. The problems we create come when we rely on how we look or how we make ourselves look as our primary tool for attracting and impressing others.

God gave us wonderful and beautiful bodies. They were not intended for manipulating others. When we make it our lifestyle to develop inward character, outward modesty, and upward devotion, we actually allow our bodies to fulfill their best purposes. Our I.O.U. continues to flourish and become even more beautiful as the years roll by, long after the physical shell has suffered the effects of time. When we base relationships on what is passing and fading, we make these relationships vulnerable to time. Instead, God offers us a revolutionary way of thinking about lasting attraction between people—the truth.

A Second Sexual Revolution Demands We Learn a New Way to Relate to the Opposite Sex

The second sexual revolution involves a new way of thinking, a new way of attracting, and a radical new way of relating to one another. Right now in the way the world relates, others are objects to capture, "true love" to find, or sources to use for sexual recreation. The world treats others more like targets than persons made in God's image. The Hollywood formula has deceived us into thinking we are the center of the universe. Everyone else, if they knew their place, would exist to serve our needs. We don't say it that crudely or even think it that specifically, but we treat others as if that was the case. Only a revolution will break the cycle of self-centeredness.

By sharp contrast, the way that God has treated us shows us at least **three revolutionary ways to relate to the opposite sex.**

---

1. Start Out as Friends

Long before we parents talk to our kids about sex, we actually need to speak often about friendship. We need to teach our kids to relate to the opposite sex as friends. John 15:13 gives us a great definition to share with our children and to follow ourselves: *"Greater love has no one than this, that he lay down his life for his friends."* That was Jesus' personal description of friendship that he lived out perfectly. Relationships with the opposite sex should be based on friendship first, not romance, not hormones, not attraction.

It occurs to me that whatever is left of the old idea of dating is probably outmoded. Is there a right time to date? I'm sure there is, but when we have fifth, sixth, seventh, and eighth graders pairing off for pseudoromances, we are actually robbing youth of great friendships and instead are enrolling them in the disappointing school of the Hollywood formula of living and loving. We don't really think children that young need to be in training for marriage. But I suggest that we are setting our children up by allowing them to get on the merry-go-round: Get emotionally connected, feel all the vibes of pseudorecreational romance, get your heart broken, give your heart away, get it broken again, give your heart away, get it broken again, get numb, learn to manipulate men, learn to manipulate women, experience the breakup cycle, and over and over.

Do you know what that dizzying repetition does? We unintentionally help our children learn that once they make a real commitment in marriage, they can expect that it probably will break up too. They've been trained in it. Instead, we all need friendship training. **What would happen if in place of the early dating focus, we talked and encouraged our children to become friends with people of the opposite sex as a healthy and mature objective?**

My guess is that you have learned the riches of friendship the hard way. I know I did. So did most of the people whose stories you've heard in these pages. I did the dating dance and saw little potential for a relationship with any woman that didn't have romantic overtones. Then I met Theresa. We were friends about a year and a half before any romantic lights came on, and the beauty of it was the circumstances helped me follow God's prescription, even though I didn't realize it at the time. Her two little boys and her situation in general made her easy to befriend. I realized she was lovely, but I assumed she was "out of bounds" and really needed a brother in Christ as a friend and encourager with the boys.

We were part of a larger circle of Christian friends. I wasn't trying to impress her or always trying to look my best. We weren't playing the game. We prayed together, shared together, worshipped together, and participated in ministry together. We learned an amazing amount about each other without the constant reminder that she was a woman and I was a man. Because we were part of a larger group, spending time together rarely involved being alone. Looking back, I realize that because our focus was on Christ and helping each other grow in him, we weren't really aware of the way we gradually grew together.

I was in Venezuela on a mission trip when I fell in love with Theresa. By then, I had known her about a year and a half. God brought her to my mind in an unexpected way. I was praying for a wife, and it was almost as if God whispered, "What about Theresa?" I clearly remember my first response: "I don't want to be a dad; I just want a wife." But after a while I had another startling revelation. God seemed to say, "Well, you've been praying for her. Maybe you're the answer." I had recently been praying that Theresa would find a suitable mate, since I felt her boys really needed a dad and her life as a single mom was incredibly difficult. Once the new possibility settled in my mind, I suddenly felt a release to allow my attraction for Theresa to grow in other ways. I discovered that almost everything that I appreciated deeply in her were the very qualities I hoped would be in the woman I married. But our well-seasoned friendship allowed us to talk honestly about the complications of jumping from single man to full-fledged dad with twins in a twinkling of an eye.

Friendship provides a wonderful playground for discovering and developing very important qualities in prospective husbands or wives, without the sometimes relentless pressure of being "on display" or "under the microscope" of the dating game. Friendship doesn't put exclusivity on a relationship. Friendship provides a very good relationship without having to move on to romance. Romance creates a relationship that hardly ever reverses to friendship. In working with college students for over ten years, I saw the beautiful fruit of what can happen when God's people are willing to make friendship rather than romance their first priority. I also saw the tragic results of making romance central.

In fact, I think we need to give careful attention to the way we move from friendship to romance. **Courtship gives us a better format than dating when it comes to laying the groundwork for marriage.** In his book *I Kissed Dating Goodbye,* Joshua Harris repeatedly emphasizes the point that a person has no right to ask for another's heart and affection unless he or she is also prepared to offer a lasting commitment.[2] This declaration expresses the underlying principles of courtship. Is there a time to date? Of course! Is it right to "pair off" to discern God's will in a serious relationship? Yes. But the research on when to date and what occurs when romance precedes friendship is both disturbing and provides an important warning to heed.

A study by the University of Utah involving 2,400 teens revealed the following statistics:

- If a young person begins dating at the age of twelve, there's a 91 percent chance that they will have sex before they graduate from high school.
- If they begin dating at thirteen, there's a 56 percent chance they will have sex before they finish high school.
- If they begin dating at the age of fourteen, there's a 53 percent chance.
- At age fifteen, it's a 40 percent chance.
- If they begin dating at sixteen, it drops all the way down to 20 percent.[3]

Those statistics send ice cubes coursing through my veins. I want to tell every mom and dad I know to hold their ground. Tell your fourteen-year-old, "No dating, son or daughter. Sorry, but we love you too much." You will have to learn to say it several ways but always include the no part. Be ready for the standard response: "Yeah, but everyone else gets to do it!" When you hear that sales pitch, remind them of the chaos and damage occurring in those relationships. Answer their frustration with a calm explanation of God's prescription for love, sex, and lasting relationships. Invite them to join the second sexual revolution. And if all else fails, you can use the line I mentioned before—the one my kids hated but later learned to believe, "I guess my no just means I love you more than all the other parents love their kids."

> Courtship gives us a better format than dating when it comes to laying the groundwork for marriage.

Encourage situations in which your kids (or you) will be relating to others in a group setting rather than pairing off. The current average age for a man in our country to get married is twenty-seven. Ten years ago that age was twenty-three, and about fifteen years before that it was probably nineteen or twenty. The average age of marriage for a woman today is twenty-three. Ten years ago it was twenty-one; thirty years ago it was around seventeen or eighteen. What do you think is going to happen to people who are in relationships that involve dealing with hormonal issues as early as age thirteen? We've allowed a pattern to develop that almost insures our children will be drawn into immorality, whatever their motives. The longer you delay the pairing up, the greater the probability they will think with their head instead of their heart or their hormones. They will need your help to do it God's way.

2. Treat Others as Brothers or Sisters in Christ

Be a revolutionary by treating the opposite sex as a family member you deeply respect. First Timothy 5:1–2 records Paul's counsel to Timothy about various relationships: *"Do not rebuke an older man harshly, but exhort him as if he were your father. Treat younger men as brothers, older women as mothers, and younger women as sisters, with absolute purity."*

Notice how he treats each relationship. Here's how to relate to older men—don't ever rebuke an older man sharply because he should receive the kind of honor and respect you give your father. Here's how to relate to older women—as mothers in the Lord. And then in verse 2 he basically says, "Treat younger women as sisters, in all purity." **What would happen in every relationship with the opposite sex among Christians if we treated people as brothers and sisters in Christ?** Aren't there some boundaries that almost automatically emerge if we treat each other as a brother or sister? I mean, think of how you treat your biological sister. Do you ever hug her? Of course. Do you hug her like you hug some other people? Of course not. Do you touch your sister or brother in ways that show affirmation and caring and genuine relationship? Yes. Are there certain ways you would never touch your brother or sister? Absolutely.

Recognizing and honoring the family bonds that we have in Christ can raise some significant protective walls in relationships. And the additional emphasis on friendship as well as family bonds in Christ will create the kind of healthy relationships in which God's prescription for love, sex, and lasting relationships can be lived out.

---

3. Make the Spiritual Growth and Well-Being of Others Your Number One Priority

In the second sexual revolution, every relationship is guided by the fact that we're fellow followers of Christ. As such, we long to see and assist each other's spiritual growth. Hebrews 10:24 says, "And let us consider how we may spur one another on toward love and good deeds." That's men, women, everybody actively and consciously seeking ways to stimulate love and good works.

Here's the primary question you can ask of every relationship: "In this relationship with my brother or sister in Christ, am I helping him or her become more and more like Christ? Further, how exactly am I seeking to gently push or even challenge him or her to a closer walk with God?" If you and I can't answer those questions clearly, the relationships we are forming are not healthy. But if our relationships are enthusiastic adventures that have as their goal to help one another walk in the light, even if our lives go separate ways, we will be able to express deep gratitude for the benefits we have shared. We will be able to say, "Thank you, sister or brother. I grew in Christ because of my friendship with you, and we have some great memories of serving Christ together."

Now, when you start going down that trail, God will see that healthy, romantic love will blossom at the right time and in the right way. The Spirit of God will show you a potential mate and then you can pair off and figure out as friends how and if to move toward marriage. As I tell young people all the time, there's a lifetime worth of amazing lessons to learn about friendship and life as brothers and sisters in the body of Christ before you need to start worrying about romantic love. Genuine love, satisfying sex, and lasting, life-giving relationships will be a reward for those who choose to live with others by God's prescription. I can't think of a better description of a wedding ceremony than a celebration of another important victory in the second sexual revolution.

Will You Sign on the Dotted Line?

So, how about you? Are you ready for the second sexual revolution? Will you join me and tens of thousands of other Christians who choose not simply to talk about our faith but to live it out in the most controversial area in our culture—our sexuality? Will your life become another radical light in the darkness?

Joining the second sexual revolution will not be easy. You will have to wade upstream through a raging flood of moral filth and pollution that seems to come from every direction in our culture. Are you ready to move against that flow, leaning into the pressure that is sure to come? Are you prepared to question the way you have been trained to think about sexuality and abandon dysfunctional attitudes that will bring chaos to your relationships? Are you willing to rebel against unhealthy living?

Further, are you ready to have your mind radically renewed and reprogrammed by God's Word to a conviction that:

- sex is sacred
- sex is serious
- sex is an awesome responsibility

Imagine what could happen as our new way of thinking leads to life-changing behaviors that become a shining light that penetrates our culture. Imagine what could happen as we implement a radical way of attracting the opposite sex and developing genuine relationships. Imagine what could happen if significant numbers of marriages began, not weighed down with the baggage of immorality but buoyed with the anticipation of unfolding a precious gift that has been kept for one other person. Imagine a healthy return to modesty outside marriage and exuberant sex within it. Imagine love, sex, and lasting relationships as God designed them, and you'll be in a revolutionary state of mind!

Personal Evaluation

1. How would you explain to someone the truth that sex is serious business to God?

2. In what specific ways do you realize you will have to change your way of thinking about sexuality in order to be part of the second sexual revolution?

3. Why do you think genuine godliness is such an attractive trait in another person?

— 4. How significant in your own life has been the presence or lack of godly friends?

— 5. What decision have you made in the core of your being about your participation in the second sexual revolution?

Conclusion

Welcome to the Revolution

At the beginning of this journey I posed some questions about the woeful status of relationships in our culture:

- Are we all destined to be frustrated and become the products and perpetrators of dysfunctional relationships?
- Or is there a better way? Is there, in fact, a secret, a plan, or a different paradigm for genuine love, great sex, and an enduring relationship?

I also made a promise to describe for you that prescription and plan. It doesn't belong to me nor did I invent it. It comes from God's Word. I've passed it on to you, not because I'm particularly smart or have an inside corner on love, sex, and lasting relationships, but because I am convinced that the One who created you to be loved and who made sex for your enjoyment actually has an understandable game plan for how relationships can and do work. I repeat the promise that if you will trust and implement this way of thinking about and doing relationships, your relationships can be deeply satisfying and lasting. As I said in the introduction, these principles work because they come from the One who designed you. Love, sex, and lasting relationships were all God's idea. He made you and me for relationship and created our longing for connection with others. Because you are the object of his love and affection, he wants to fulfill these longings in ways beyond your wildest dreams.

> I repeat the promise that if you will trust and implement this way of thinking about and doing relationships, your relationships can be deeply satisfying and lasting.

There are two ways to do relationships: Hollywood's way and God's way. We can follow the world's formula and get the world's results, or we can accept God's prescription and experience his blessing on our lives. The choice may not be easy, but it's very clear. That choice is always before us, whether we are young or old, single or married for many years. **We can exchange one way of doing relationships for the other at any time, but the results will always be related to the choices we make.**

A Closing Story

I want to close with a true story. This person's experience reminds us that no matter who we are or where we have been, God wants to forgive, restore, and reconstruct our relational world. It also reminds us that the choice we make will have lasting effects. Read the following account slowly and hear both the warning and the hope that's available for you.

Over the years I've received hundreds of heartbreaking confirmations that people are hungry to hear this message about the need for a second sexual revolution. Even more troubling have been the conversations with people who are dealing with the painful aftereffects of the Hollywood formula. I'm hoping one more story from the other side of the experience will help you answer God's call in your life for a second sexual revolution. As you read this confession that was e-mailed to me, ask yourself, *What are the implications for me—as a parent, married mate, divorced, or a single person? What are the implications for my lifestyle? What are the implications for how I'm going to relate and think when it comes to the opposite sex?* Let the following account of a man's relational decisions help you analyze your life once more:

> I accepted the Lord in high school and was on fire for God through college into my midtwenties, but then I fell away from God, big time. I got involved in three consecutive relationships with women at work. In each of those relationships, the women got pregnant but with my encouragement went through abortions. Three kids I helped to conceive never had a chance to take their first breath. Wouldn't you know it? All three relationships dissolved soon after the abortions. It amazes me now that I couldn't see the pattern I was creating.
>
> Here I am now, a number of years later, greatly blessed in marriage to a Christ-centered woman, and we've been unable to have children of our own. It's been devastating to me in light of having paid with my own money to kill three babies of my own. Was sex fun? No question. Was the pleasure worth the price I have paid? I can't scream "NO" loudly enough.
>
> Like you said, the deepest desire in my heart was to have a committed lasting relationship. But I didn't get anywhere near that in any of the flings that I had. As bad as the situation got, I still didn't learn my lesson. My next step away from God's way came with a girlfriend that I moved in with. She had two children already. The relationship we developed was truly evil. She didn't want to have anything to do with spiritual issues. I sacrificed any integrity that I may have had left, and I failed to stand for the truth in my day-to-day life with her. It was a degrading and unsatisfying relationship, and believe me, it definitely messed with those kids' heads. What kind of example was I setting?
>
> Thankfully, the Spirit of God interceded. I came to my senses and realized I had a decision to make. I was at a fork in the road. Thankfully, I discovered God's prescription for love, sex, and lasting relationships. I trashed the Hollywood formula that had guided my

chaotic life. And God has worked a miracle of healing and guidance in my life. Yes, I have regrets, but I also have God's grace. Now the only possible reason for mentioning my past mistakes is to perhaps encourage others to avoid the same mistakes or turn away from the life they are already living apart from God's way. Thanks be to God, I was a twentieth-century prodigal son who ran to God without ever looking back, and I've been in fellowship with the Lord and believers ever since. By the grace of God, my wife and I have been blessed to adopt a baby, yet it still grieves me to think of the mistakes I made with those past relationships. Please keep sharing the good news that God has a much better way to experience love, sex, and lasting relationships.

The man who wrote that note made a wise and painful choice. The same choice lies before you today. You can stay on the same path to continue the destruction, or you can make a radical turn and head right back to God; it's your choice. Perhaps as you have read this book, a mental picture has gradually formed of a fork in the road. Which fork will you choose? Which way is your family going to go? If you want real love, great sex, and lasting relationships, you'll make it your purpose to follow God's prescription. You will never regret the choice!

My Prayer for You

Father, thank you for loving us. Thank you that your Word in the Book of Ephesians was written to a group of people whose sexual mores and chaos were far worse than ours. Thank you for showing us through their example that, as impossible as it sounds to our twenty-first-century ears, we too can live out this radical life that transformed the world. Thank you that the same power that raised Christ from the dead lives in us and enables us to be pure. We gratefully acknowledge that the Christian life is not about trying hard but about the fact that you have given us the grace and the power in Christ to follow you with all of our heart.

Help us think differently about our sexuality, help us to attract others with integrity and honesty, and help us to relate in truthful and helpful ways with each other. Give us your strength to become the right kind of people, to grow and walk in love, to fix our hope on you and walk in your light. Give us the quiet courage to participate in the second sexual revolution in our culture. In Christ's name. Amen.

Notes

Chapter 1

1. *New York Times Almanac: 1999*, ed. John W. Wright (New York: Penguin, 1998), 351.

2. Judith Wollerstein, "Children of Divorce, Twenty-Five Years Later," *USA Weekend*, September 2000, 15–17

Chapter 4

1. Les and Leslie Parrott, *Relationships* (Grand Rapids: Zondervan, 1998), 134.

Chapter 6

1. Parrott, *Relationships*, 131.
2. Ibid., 132.
3. Ibid., 132–33.
4. Paula Rinehart, "Losing Our Promiscuity," *Christianity Today*, 10 July 2000, 32–33.
5. Ibid.

Chapter 8

1. Bethesda Research Group, in William R. Mattox Jr., "The Hottest Valentine," *Washington Post*, 1994.

2. M. D. Newcomb and P. M. Bentler, "Assessment of Personality and Demographic Aspects of Cohabitation and Marital Success," *Journal of Personality Assessment* 44 (1980): 21.

3. L. H. Bukstel, G. D. Roeder, P. R. Kilmann, J. Laughlin, and W. Sotile, "Projected Extramarital Sexual Involvement in Unmarried College Students," *Journal of Marriage and the Family* 40 (1978): 337–40.

4. Parrott, *Relationships*, 138.

5. Ibid., 139.

Chapter 10

1. Wendy Shalit, *A Return to Modesty* (New York: The Free Press, 1999), 209. See also Rinehart, "Losing Our Promiscuity," for several significant quotes from Wendy.

2. Joshua Harris, *I Kissed Dating Goodbye* (Sisters, Ore.: Multnomah, 1997).

3. University of Utah study on teens engaging in premarital sex related to age of starting to date.

Chip Ingram (Th.M., Dallas Theological Seminary) is president and CEO of Walk Thru the Bible in Atlanta, Georgia. His popular radio program, *Living on the Edge,* can be heard on hundreds of stations nationwide and on the Internet (www.lote.org). Chip and his wife, Theresa, are the parents of three sons and one daughter.

ALSO IN AUDIO

Bakeraudio on Compact Disc

LOVE, SEX, AND LASTING RELATIONSHIPS

GOD'S PRESCRIPTION FOR ENHANCING YOUR LOVE LIFE

CHIP INGRAM

A FRESH APPROACH FOR THOSE WHO DESIRE MEANINGFUL, LIFELONG RELATIONSHIPS

290 minutes (4 CDs)

Many couples struggle to have a meaningful relationship and seem clueless when it comes to making it last. Yet they crave a quality love life that goes beyond physical attraction.

Those who have heard Chip Ingram's teaching and radio ministry on the subjects of love, sex, and lasting relationships have reported significant help as a result of their exposure to the principles he draws from God's Word. In this audio book, listeners will hear why many relationships fail and discover the principles they need for breaking the trend. The CDs combine biblical teaching, sociological research, and personal stories, often challenging widely held beliefs about how to establish and maintain healthy relationships.

Winsome but straightforward, this engaging audio book provides a new lens through which to look at the opposite sex and practical, specific ways to build the kind of relationships that last.

ALSO BY CHIP INGRAM

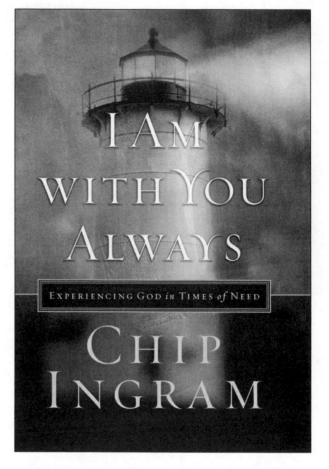

Do you long to experience God today? Maybe you need a fresh encounter with your heavenly Father because you're gripped by fear, troubled by a crisis or transition, or simply feeling that life has handed you a raw deal.

In *I Am with You Always,* pastor Chip Ingram explores pivotal chapters in the Psalms, revealing how you can meet God in the midst of your most difficult moments. Chip's candid discussion of today's most pressing needs, as well as personal stories and solid guidance, will allow you to move from "knowing about God" to profoundly experiencing his presence and power in your life. You'll be reminded that the Lord is faithful to hear your heart's cry and will be there for you, time and again.

"I DON'T WANT YOU MERELY GETTING FRESH IDEAS ABOUT GOD.
WHAT I REALLY WANT IS FOR YOU TO ENCOUNTER
THE LIVING GOD AS HE REVEALS HIMSELF TO YOU."

—CHIP INGRAM

CONTENTS